Engineer THIS!

Engineer THIS!

10 Amazing Projects for Young Mechanical Engineers

Prufrock Press Inc.

Carol J. McBride & Francisco L. Gonzales

Illustrations by Eliza Bolli • Photos by Michael Samaripa

Library of Congress Cataloging-in-Publication Data

Names: McBride, Carol, 1955- author. | Gonzales, Francisco L., 1957- author.
Title: Engineer this! : 10 amazing projects for young mechanical engineers /
    by Carol J. McBride and Francisco L. Gonzales ; edited by Katy McDowall.
Description: Waco, Texas : Prufrock Press Inc., 2017. | Includes
    bibliographical references.
Identifiers: LCCN 2017025850 | ISBN 9781618216298 (pbk.)
Subjects: LCSH: Machinery--Amateurs' manuals--Juvenile literature. |
    Mechanical engineering--Juvenile literature.
Classification: LCC TJ147 .M349 2017 | DDC 621--dc23
LC record available at https://lccn.loc.gov/2017025850

Edited by Katy McDowall

Cover and layout design by Raquel Trevino
Illustrations by Eliza Bolli
Photos by Michael Samaripa

ISBN-13: 978-1-61821-629-8

Printed in the United States of America.

At the time of this book's publication, all facts and figures cited are the most current available. All telephone numbers, addresses, and website URLs are accurate and active. All publications, organizations, websites, and other resources exist as described in the book, and all have been verified. The authors and Prufrock Press Inc. make no warranty or guarantee concerning the information and materials given out by organizations or content found at websites, and we are not responsible for any changes that occur after this book's publication. If you find an error, please contact Prufrock Press Inc.

Prufrock Press Inc.
P.O. Box 8813
Waco, TX 76714-8813
Phone: (800) 998-2208
Fax: (800) 240-0333
http://www.prufrock.com

Table of Contents

Acknowledgements

Misa Gonzales and Cassie Gonzales, our daughters, grew up knee-deep in engineering, arts and crafts, design, and problem solving. We were always the Four Musketeers, in this together, innovating, inventing, and designing. Our grandchildren, Zavier Gonzales and Krysma Bousquet, have carried on the tradition.

Introduction

Engineer This! offers 10 hands-on projects that will sharpen your engineering eye, expanding your knowledge of math, engineering, and science concepts. The projects will help you discover the various real-world principles that make machines work! Instead of simply memorizing abstract concepts like *kinetic energy* and *potential energy*, you will learn about and use them as you build completely functional machines.

From gliders and motorcars to parachutes and egg-laying ducks, you will use science, engineering, and your own problem-solving skills and creativity. As you build a glider, you will explore the elements of flight, including gravity, thrust, lift, and drag. And, as you build a motorcar, you will experiment with different body materials in order to build the fastest vehicle.

Throughout, you will learn to solve problems in creative ways. You will learn to experiment and change your perspective to see if you can help something work even better. Sometimes you will change the shape of the nose of your glider, or you might add weight to it to see if it flies better. You also might try turning it upside down to fly it. Each project will challenge you to hypothesize, learn from failure, explore alternative methods and materials for success, and—more than that—think just like an engineer.

How to Use this Book

Each project has its own section. The projects increase in difficulty as you progress through the book. For example, the bat wings are the simplest project, whereas the motorcar is the most difficult. Rest assured, however, as each project includes detailed step-by-step instructions, a comprehensive list of materials and tools, and troubleshooting tips for success. Projects also include full-color photos, safety guidelines, and extended engineering and science activities and experiments. There's also a glossary at the end of the book, which includes helpful definitions of many terms as well as suggestions for successfully working with particular materials.

Safety

Most of these projects require close adult supervision. You will often be cutting with tools much sharper and stronger than scissors. There may also be harmless, mild sparks if a project requires batteries and electrical connections. As much as possible, you want to be able to do all of the steps yourself, but if you have any questions about whether you are capable of doing something that is potentially harmful, always err on the side of safety. When in doubt, ask a parent or responsible adult for assistance. Also keep in mind that you don't have to work alone. You may want to partner with a friend and put your heads together to figure out how to make your machine work.

Here are a few more safety guidelines:

1. You are responsible for safety when working alone or with others.

2. You are responsible for safety when using tools or helping others use tools.

3. Safe use of equipment and tools includes handling tools correctly, not playing with the tools, and not playing around anyone using tools.

4. When using a glue gun, always use a low-temperature mini glue gun. Wherever and whenever possible, put hot glue on the larger object as you glue things together.

5. Do not put hot glue on thinner plastics, such as soda or water bottles. The plastic will melt and warp. When decorating on plastics, put the glue on the paper or wood and let it cool for a few seconds and then stick it onto the softer plastic.

6. You must be observant, considerate, and aware of what others around you are doing.

7. Always share tools, space, and knowledge!

Materials and Tools

For the most part, the materials listed for each project are easy to find and inexpensive. Many can be found in your recycling bin, such as toilet paper rolls, egg cartons, and cereal boxes. Others may be lying around the house or need to be purchased, including motors, AA batteries, paint, and other materials to decorate your projects.

You will need a variety of tools for completing projects. Tools are anything used to make changes: a pencil, a pen, markers, crayons, a low-temperature mini glue gun, single hole punch, diagonal cutting pliers, needle-nose pliers, rulers,

Think about this!
Whenever a project calls for decorations or for you to design your own creature, it's your chance to get creative!

craft scissors, and more. Most projects require the use of adult-size craft scissors and a low-temperature mini glue gun and glue sticks. Several projects require more specialized tools available at craft or hardware stores. Your parent or guardian may know where to find them. You may even have some of them in your own garage already. These include:

- ✓ diagonal cutting pliers for the bobbing dog, rubber band-propelled car, catapult, and egg-laying creature;
- ✓ needle-nose pliers for the bat wings, rubber band-propelled car, and motorcar;
- ✓ a hammer and nail for the motorcar;
- ✓ a hacksaw for the motorcar; and
- ✓ wire strippers for the motorcar.

Think about this!

Anthropologists sometimes find tools developed by early humans. Consider the stone tools found in 2011 near Lake Turkana, Kenya, formerly known as Lake Rudolph (Choi, 2015). The tools were more than 3.3 million years old! Early human ancestors made the tools in order to eat nuts, insects, and meat by breaking, bashing, and cutting.

How important are these tools? They were fabricated for a purpose, not just found and used, such as wielding a rock as a hammer to break nutshells. *Fabricating* (or engineering) these tools involved striking a rock against another rock, chipping away at it until the second rock was sharp enough to cut meat.

You won't be creating your own tools—but you might be glad someone did!

Concepts and Skills

The projects will broaden your understanding of a number of math and science concepts and skills.

Simple and Complex Machines

Simple machines help us do work. The lever, screw, wedge, inclined plane, wheel and axle, and pulley are all *simple machines*. These are the six classic simple machines identified by Renaissance scientists. When force is applied to simple machines, they do work. The *wheel and axle* move goods and people. The *lever and fulcrum* are the seesaw that moves up and down, a crane that lifts steel beams, or a swinging door. The *wedge* separates things; it's a knife or nail. A *ramp* or *inclined plane* allows us to move weight uphill or downhill. *Pulleys* move objects up and down. A *screw* fastens things together or transports water uphill.

A *complex machine* is two or more simple machines working together. All machines have a combination of these simple machines. For example, the shovel is a simple machine—a lever. The mechanical post-hole digger is a complex machine with two levers, whereas the gas-powered post-hole digger is a complex machine with a screw, lever, fulcrum, wheel, and axle.

Engineering Design

You are probably already comfortable with the scientific method of research and discovery. Although the engineering design process is similar, its main emphasis is on creativity, design, and innovation.

As an engineer, the kinds of questions you ask yourself depend on what problems you are trying to solve. Some of the questions you might ask yourself include:

- ✓ Is engineering design needed for this project?
- ✓ Is this project considered progress—does it build upon and improve existing ideas?
- ✓ Can I reproduce it for manufacturing?
- ✓ Will it hold up over the time it is needed?
- ✓ Will the materials always be available? If not, what material changes must be made?

The engineering design process has a variety of steps and versions. Below, five common steps—ask, imagine, plan, create, and improve—are listed (Engineering is Elementary, 2017). Using the rubber band-propelled car as an example, each step listed includes examples of the kinds of considerations you might make as you work on the projects in this book. There may be more things that you need to consider as you work on a project, but this is the bare minimum of things you need to think about when designing.

1. **Ask:** What is the problem? What are my limits? Materials? Workspace needed? How long will it take to build it? What are the skills needed?

   > *I wanted to build a rubber band-propelled car. I wanted to build it out of the recyclables and craft supplies at my house. The car needs to be able to zoom across the floor; it should be durable enough so someone can play with it over and over again; it has to be easy to repair; and, finally, decorating the car should not restrict its function as a very fast, rubber band-propelled car.*

2. **Imagine:** What is possible? Brainstorm ideas with others. Or, you can come up with a list of possible rubber band-propelled car designs by yourself.

> *I had large plastic water, soda, and juice bottles; cardboard; chopsticks; and plastic lids, so I created a design using my most durable materials that were also lightweight and structurally tough. I believe I chose the best idea.*

3. **Plan:** Sketch out a design, and then list the materials you will need, along with the tools and the time you think it will take to create it.

> *The plastic soda bottle design with four large plastic lids was an easy sketch and helped me to understand possible problems. If the lids/wheels are too big, they can rub against each other and operate the same way brakes work on a car, as friction between two objects. I made a list and gathered my tools.*

4. **Create:** Follow a plan, adjusting and changing as soon as problems arise. Problem solving is part of the creative process.

> *My front wheels wouldn't turn. There was a barely visible hot glue string stretching from the wheel to the side of the bottle. Easy solution: The string was cold and brittle, so I wiped the string away.*

5. **Improve:** How can you make your design better? You may not see all of the possibilities until your project is built and tested.

Stretchier rubber bands? The car's back wheels were spinning too fast and not getting enough traction with the floor. I put extra weight on the rear of the car to add traction to the wheels. When the wheels grip the floor, the car can go faster and farther.

Learning From Real-Life Engineers

As you work through each project, you will be asked to work just like a real-life engineer.

Materials engineers. Consider *materials engineers*, who analyze materials, discover new materials, and realign the properties of materials all the way down to their atomic structure. An important property could be strength, like steel or titanium, or weather-resistant polycarbonates and their malleability. These engineers change the way the materials are used and how they react to heat, cold, and stress. Materials engineers also develop biodegradable materials, the way cardboard or paper decomposes over time. The ongoing impact on the environment is always important along with the cost of producing and maintaining the product.

When you select your materials, like the plastic bottle for the rubber band-propelled car, you will choose it based on your engineering needs: size, structural strength, malleability (is it thin enough to cut?), and availability.

Mechanical engineers. *Mechanical engineering* uses principles of mechanics, physics, computer technology, and materials to design, create, and maintain machines. The mechanical projects you build will need to last and be repaired; they will spin, zoom, seesaw, and/or glide. The decisions you make will determine how fast or slow a project spins, the amount of sway in the balance of the seesaw, and how high, fast, smooth, or in which direction your machine will glide.

Civil engineers. *Civil engineering* is the design and construction of roads, bridges, canals, dams, and buildings. These engineers were involved in the oldest engineering discipline—military engineering—followed by public works: bridges, roads, and dams.

Think about this!
What types of engineering need expanding? Solar energy engineering? Engineering with recycled materials?

When building the bobbing dog, the creature that lays an egg, and all of the other projects that need to last through time and use, you will need to answer civil engineering questions. What kind of pressure and stress are you subjecting the projects to?

Structural engineers. *Structural engineering* is designing buildings, bridges, and any structures that have to support a lot of weight and resist weather. These engineers must design structures that can stand up to hurricanes, rain, snow, weight, and deterioration over time. Structural engineers also design cars and trucks so that

Think about this!
What other types of engineering can you see being used in these projects?

they crinkle up and take the impact of a crash. Along with seatbelts and airbags, collapsing of the vehicle allows the occupants to survive uninjured or with minor injuries.

Consider the creature that lays an egg: It has to be strong enough to withstand constant compressing. Pushing down on its back puts stress on the rubber bands, the animal's legs, and its torso.

Renewable energy engineers. These engineers are involved in environmentally friendly engineering that involves renewable, geothermal, and alternative energies. *Renewable energy* is sun, wind, rain, and geothermal. *Geothermal* is steam that comes from under the Earth's surface. *Alternative energy* is energy that is not fossil fuel (usually includes biofuels, solar, wind, and steam). The rubber band in the bat wings project is considered alternative energy.

Think about this!
As you work on a project, consider this: How economical and ecological will your finished product be over time?

Getting Started

The most important thing to remember as you begin to build projects is this: Don't be afraid to fail. Gliders will crash. Parachutes may not open. Bobbing dogs may not bob. Your goal is to create fully functional machines, but things may not always go according to plan. These simple machines may challenge you. You will likely have to tweak your designs in order to succeed—just like an engineering professional.

Each project involves quality, precise work. For example, the rubber band-propelled car only works if the wheels are perfectly aligned. If they aren't, the car will go in a circle. The glider will fly only if the wings are designed well, if the body and wings achieve a balance of sorts, if they are constructed out of the right materials, and if the pieces are cut correctly.

Sometimes, however, the projects will surprise you. Consider the designs of the wings on the glider, for example. Sometimes the large clunky wings that you might think will crash and burn carry the glider in a graceful glide across the room much farther than the more streamlined designs.

Best of luck as you go forth. Wherever your engineering creations take you, remember: Dream big, create, experiment, and have fun!

Think about this!

As you work, document each step you take. Record your step-by-step building process and the changes you make to the design. Engineers document their process so they:

✓ don't repeat their mistakes,
✓ can duplicate their successes, and
✓ can easily make future repairs.

Projects

Bat wings

Supplies

- ❑ Large steel paper clip
- ❑ 3/4-inch by 1 1/4-inch (or smaller) piece of corrugated cardboard (or foam core)
- ❑ Two size #16 rubber bands
- ❑ Size #10 envelope
- ❑ Decorations (paint, markers, construction paper, etc.)

> **Think about this!**
> Some rubber bands can be too stretchy. You will need to find what works for you.

Tools

- ❑ Needle-nose pliers
- ❑ Adult-size craft scissors
- ❑ Hole punch

What Should Happen

You will stretch and unwind a paper clip wire into a right angle. Then, you will loop two rubber bands through a hole in a cardboard rectangle and attach the rubber bands to the paper clip. This will allow you to wind the cardboard rectangle tightly enough

> **Think about this!**
> What is (are) the simple machine(s) in the bat wings project?

for it to leap off of the table. Wind it back up, stick it in an envelope, and hand it to a friend. It should leap out when the envelope is opened!

INSTRUCTIONS

1. Carefully unroll (don't twist) a paper clip (see diagram 1a) until it looks like an L (see diagram 1b).

2. Use needle-nose pliers to twist the ends of the paper clip inward into loops (see diagram 2).

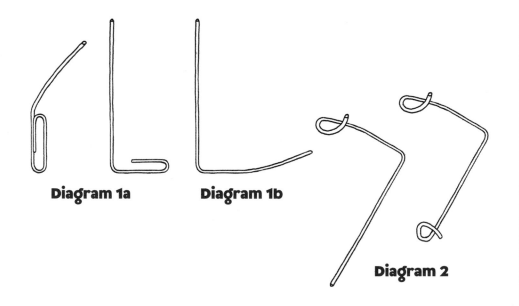

Diagram 1a   **Diagram 1b**

Diagram 2

3. With a hole punch, punch a hole in the middle of your corrugated cardboard (see diagram 3). You may need an adult to help you with this step. Color or paint the rectangle if desired.

4. Insert two rubber bands into the hole (see diagram 4).

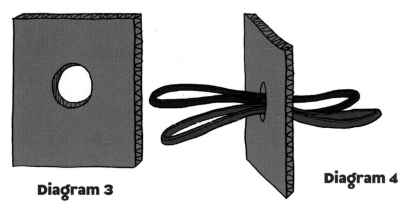

Diagram 3

Diagram 4

5. Separate the rubber bands. Pull the ends of each rubber band to the side like butterfly wings (see diagram 5).

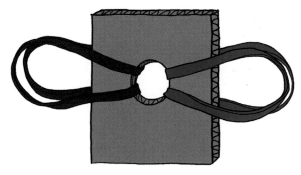

Diagram 5

Think about this!

A rubber band is considered *alternative energy*. What is alternative energy? Why is a rubber band considered alternative energy? The bat wing is like a paddle wheel, but it is powered by a rubber band instead of steam or electric. Brainstorm two other uses for the paddle wheel.

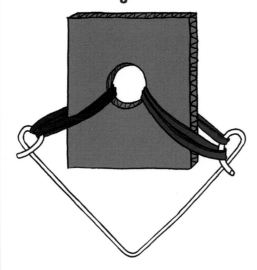

6. Attach the two loops of each rubber band to one loop of the bent paper clip (see diagram 6a). Test the apparatus: Wind the rubber bands by turning the cardboard (see diagram 6b). Let go of the cardboard. It should unwind easily.

Diagram 6a

Diagram 6b

Think about this!

With applied force, a lever moves an object at a pivot point. Where does the force come from in the bat wings? Think about a screwdriver or a door hinge, two very different levers. What are three other levers in your everyday life?

7. Decorate an envelope with a bat or other winged creature like the envelope on page 14.

8. Wind up the bat wings again, and then place the device in the envelope. Hold the outside of the envelope so that you are also holding the bat wings still. Hand the envelope to someone with the open end of the envelope toward you; the person will have to clasp the envelope right at the bat wings. If she has a good grip on the bat wings inside the envelope, then the wings will not unwind until she looks inside and the wings spring out.

Think about this!

There are more than 1,200 different species of bats. Bats are mammals—the only mammals that can actually fly instead of glide. What are some other creatures that could fly out of the envelope?

Warning!

When opening the envelope, do not put envelope close to anyone's face, including your own.

Troubleshoot This!

✓ If the cardboard doesn't unwind easily, or if the cardboard is stuck behind the paper clip, it may be too big; trim its edges.

✓ If the rubber band is too stretchy, then try a different rubber band.

✓ Adjust the shape of the paper clip so it does not rub against the cardboard.

Think about this!

Potential energy is energy that is stored in an object. Stretch a rubber band. That is potential energy. Keep stretching the rubber band to increase its potential energy. Release the rubber band, and let it shoot across the room. When it is in motion, instead of potential energy, there is kinetic energy.

Experiment With This!

✓ The energy created by the rubber band unwinding causes the cardboard rectangle to move like a paddle. The paddle motion throws the bat wings out of the envelope. What happens if you wind the rubber bands too tightly? Loosely?

✓ Change rubber bands. Try a variety of lengths and elasticity. Keep in mind: Some rubber bands are too stretchy!

✓ What other materials can you use to create a bat wing? Can you change the envelope to a box, use a spring instead of a rubber band, or replace the cardboard? Why, or why not, will the alternate material(s) work?

✓ Cut out three different shapes you can make from the cardboard instead of a rectangle. Test the shapes.

✓ How could the bat wings be made into a larger machine? Describe how these machines can be used in designing new energy or alternative energy sources.

Think about this!

The principle design of the paddle for the bat wings, the use of impellers, can be found in high-compression jet engines, hydroelectric power plants, and water pumps. Impellers are protrusions around an axle used to generate force or receive force.

Parachute

Supplies

- ❑ Plastic grocery bag
- ❑ Four 12-inch pieces of yarn
- ❑ Masking tape
- ❑ Clothespin
- ❑ Decorations (paint, markers, etc.)

Tools

- ❑ Adult-size craft scissors
- ❑ Low-temperature mini-glue gun and glue sticks or white glue

Think about this!

Round parachutes are used for descent, for landing slowly. The early designs oscillated. The vibration made them unstable and unpredictable. So, over time, a hole was designed into the apex, the uppermost top, and then the jumper had more control. Rectangular parachutes are gliders. The shape allows them to move through the air for greater distances, and the jumper has more control (Wikipedia, 2017).

What Should Happen

You will cut a circle out of a plastic bag to form a parachute. Then, you will attach four pieces of yarn and decorate a clothespin (your parachuter) to act as a ballast. You will clip the clothespin onto the yarn. This will allow you to carefully fold the parachute and throw it in to the air. Watch it open and float down!

INSTRUCTIONS

1. Cut the plastic grocery bag along the sides and across the bottom so you have two separate halves (see diagram 1).

Diagram 1

2. Find the center of one half, not counting the handles (see diagram 2).

3. Pinch the middle with your thumb and fingers and smooth the plastic down (see diagram 3).

Diagram 2

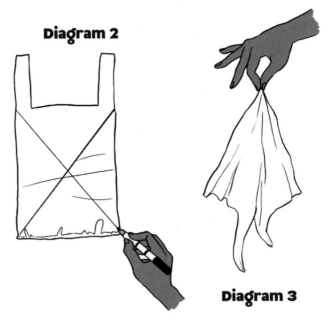

Diagram 3

4. Double-check your folds (the edges of the bag should be even) to make sure that you are holding onto the center of the plastic. Squeeze the handle end together, and then cut straight across (see diagram 4).

5. Open the piece you have remaining. It should be a perfectly round circle (see diagram 5).

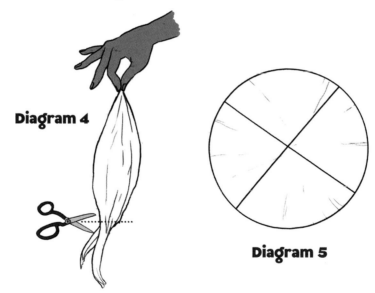

Diagram 4

Diagram 5

6. Cut four 12-inch sections of yarn (see diagram 6).

Diagram 6

7. Tape the strings to four equidistant points on the edge of the circle (see diagram 7). The tape will be on the inside of the parachute. Be sure to press the tape securely down so that none of the sticky side of the tape is exposed. Otherwise, the tape will catch the edges of the parachute and it will not open.

Diagram 7

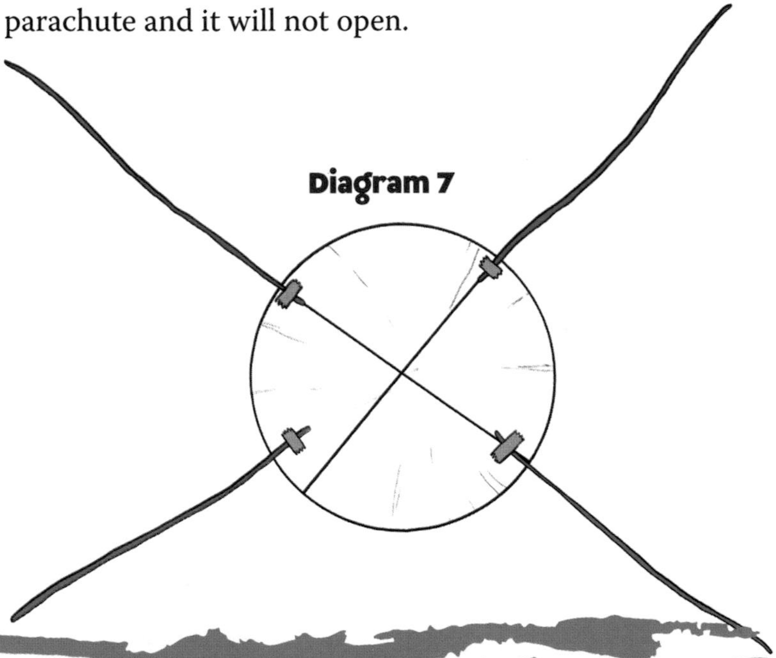

Think about this!

Early parachutes varied from umbrellas to conical shapes. They were not very effective. The parachute was improved upon primarily for military uses around World War I. The design became larger, with air holes at the apex, and a soft pack and pull cord so the user was away from the airplane before the parachute was released. A smaller parachute called a pilot chute is deployed first and pulls the larger parachute from the soft backpack (Wikipedia, 2017).

8. Decorate the clothespin you will use as a parachuter. Paint and add features (see diagram 8).

Diagram 8

9. Twist the ends of the yarn together. Clip the clothespin on the twisted yarn (see diagram 9).

Diagram 9

10. Pinch the center of the circle and smooth the edges to close the parachute. Fold it up so you can throw it into the air. Do not wrap the string around the parachute. Throw it into the air and watch it float down (see diagram 10).

Diagram 10

Think about this!

Why does the parachute float? Air resistance. Gravity, the force that holds everything on Earth, pulls the parachute to the ground. It looks like it is resisting gravity, but it is actually floating more slowly because of air resistance. The parachute, for its weight, is covering a wider space, so it floats slowly on the air—a lot slower than an unopened parachute would. The air is full of gases, like the oxygen we breathe.

Air slows a parachute or lifts a flying airplane by pushing the gases, our oxygen, to the sides. Fan your arms up and down. Feel the air? That is why a parachute floats.

Air resistance

Gravity

Troubleshoot This!

✓ If your parachute doesn't open, check your strings to make sure they are not tangled. If they aren't, throw it higher into the air to give it more time to open.

✓ Don't tie the strings together, just twist them a little and clip the clothespin onto the twist.

✓ When the yarn tangles, unclip the clothespin, straighten your yarn, retwist the ends, reclip the clothespin, and keep trying.

Experiment With This!

✓ What other materials can you use to create the parachute or the clothespin ballast? Why? Why not? Will the alternate material(s) work?

✓ Test various sizes of parachutes, parachuters, and different lengths of yarn.

Glider

Supplies

- ❑ Sturdy, 1/8- to 1/4-inch thick corrugated cardboard (or foam core) for glider body and launcher
- ❑ Wooden ruler or similarly sized piece of wood for launcher (optional)
- ❑ Cereal box (or similar type of cardboard)
- ❑ Masking tape
- ❑ Size #18 rubber band
- ❑ Decorations (paint, etc.)

Tools

- ❑ Adult-size craft scissors
- ❑ Marker or pencil
- ❑ Low-temperature mini-glue gun and glue sticks or white glue
- ❑ Paintbrush

Think about this!

A *glider* is an aircraft that is heavier than air, is aerodynamic, and does not use an engine for flight.

What Should Happen

You will cut a cardboard glider body and add wings and a rubber band. Then, you will hook the rubber band onto a launcher. Aim up and away from everyone and everything. Stretch the rubber band. Pull back on the glider and let go! It will glide through the air.

INSTRUCTIONS

1. Cut a 1 1/2 inch- to 4-inch-wide strip about 12 inches long out of corrugated cardboard or foam core (see diagram 1). This will act as the glider's body.

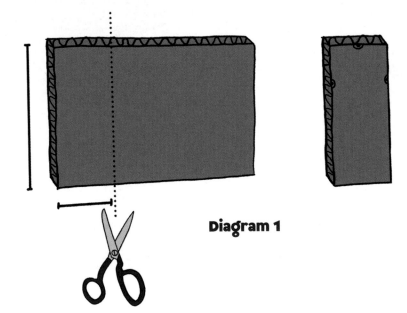

Diagram 1

2. With a maker or pencil, draw a pointed or rounded tip on one end of the glider body (see diagram 2a). Cut carefully along the line (see diagram 2b).

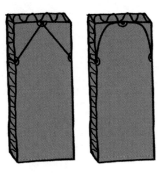

Diagram 2a   **Diagram 2b**

3. Draw your wings onto a cereal box (see diagram 3). Cut them out.

Diagram 3

Think about this!

You can make wings from a variety of household materials, including paper plates and polystyrene grocery trays. The material just needs to be strong, lightweight, and easy to cut. Pick a shape that you think will allow your glider to fly the farthest. What will work best for your glider?

4. Apply a small amount of glue to the top of the glider body (see diagram 4a). Press the wings into the glue (see diagram 4b). Tape the wings with masking tape (see diagram 4c).

Warning!

Do not put the wings on the bottom of your glider.

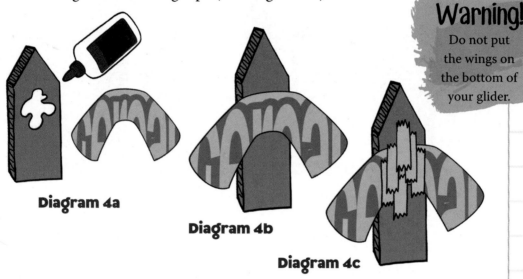

Diagram 4a

Diagram 4b

Diagram 4c

5. Tape crosswise over the first layer of tape to prevent it from pulling loose (see diagram 5).

Think about this!

Taping crosswise over your original tape will prevent it from pulling loose. How does the tape make your glider structurally stronger?

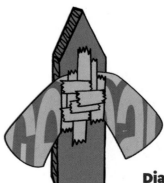

Diagram 5

6. Place a rubber band on the underside of the glider. Put at least two long pieces of tape through the rubber band. (see diagram 6).

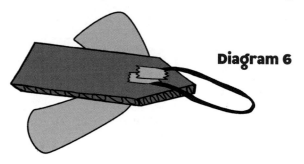

Diagram 6

7. Tape over the ends of your tape to keep the rubber band from flying off (see diagram 7). Test the rubber band. Any give? Add more tape.

Diagram 7

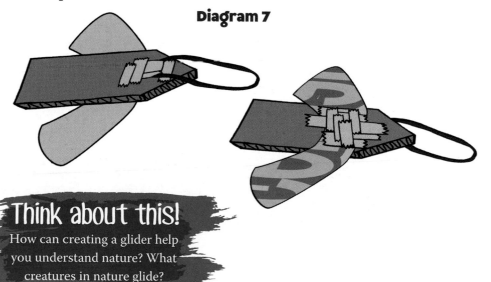

Think about this!

How can creating a glider help you understand nature? What creatures in nature glide?

8. To make a structurally strong launcher, glue two rectangles of cardboard together (see diagram 8a and 8b). Or, you can use a wooden ruler as your launcher.

Diagram 8a

Diagram 8b

9. Grip the launcher with one hand. With your other hand, hook the rubber band onto the edge of the ruler/launcher (see diagram 9). Pull back as far as you can, point the launcher and the glider up toward the sky, and let go.

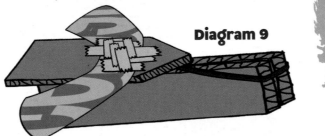

Diagram 9

Warning!
Do not point the glider at anyone while launching.

10. Paint and decorate the glider. It could be a jet fighter or a bird, such as an eagle or a macaw.

Think about this!

Four things that affect the way your glider flies through the air are: gravity, thrust, lift, and drag.

Gravity is the force caused by the rotation of the planet that wants to pull your glider to the ground. The *thrust* comes from your launching it with the rubber band. *Lift* occurs when air flows under the flat surfaces of the glider, creating a greater force than what gravity has on it. The glider will fly higher and longer if you design the wings longer and wider to create a large flat surface for the air to affect. A horseshoe shape also works well. Why? *Drag* occurs when elements of the glider, such as its shape and thickness, cause the air to work in opposition to the elements that lift it. The glider slows. You can help it fly faster by streamlining it—by not adding elements that may catch the air, keeping it from going freely over and under the glider. By understanding these elements, you can design your glider to soar higher, longer, and farther.

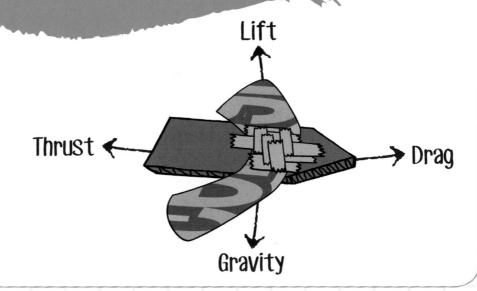

Troubleshoot This!

✓ Sometimes, a penny taped to the front end of the glider will act as a ballast and increase the weight on its nose and allow the glider to fly faster and straighter.

Experiment With This!

✓ Try different designs: bigger wings, smaller wings, wider wings, or skinnier wings. What if they are a triangle-shape like a stealth fighter? What about a bigger or smaller glider body? Use the chart on the following page to record your results.

✓ Change the angle, up or down, of one of your glider's wings. What happened? What works better?

✓ Test elasticity. Try switching rubber bands. Record the differences as you launch your glider.

✓ Add structural details and decorations to the top of your glider. Add fins. Test-fly it before and after adding parts to see which additions work best. Record the results.

Test Flight Record

Materials, Shape, and Size Used	Time in Flight	Distance

Clown-in-the-Box

Supplies

- ❑ Paper milk carton
- ❑ Strong plastic bottle
- ❑ Masking tape
- ❑ Brass fastener (brad)
- ❑ Decorations (construction paper, paint, etc.)

Think about this!

The original jack-in-the-box toy did not have a clown jumping out of it. It was a devil! Sir John Schorne of England, who lived during the medieval period, is often credited with creating the jack-in-the-box. Old carvings show him holding a boot with a devil character in it (Swenson, 2017).

Tools

- ❑ Adult-size craft scissors
- ❑ Marker
- ❑ Low-temperature mini-glue gun and glue sticks
- ❑ Paintbrush
- ❑ X-Acto knife or utility blade
- ❑ Single hole punch

What Should Happen

You will cut a paper milk carton into a box shape with a pop-up lid. Then, you will cut two plastic strips from a plastic bottle and attach them to the box base and its lid. You will create a lightweight clown or scary creature and attach the clown to the plastic strips. Finally, you will make a simple latch. The box should open with a bounce just like a jack-in-the-box!

INSTRUCTIONS

1. Draw a line around three sides of the milk carton, and then up both sides of the fourth side (see diagram 1a). This fourth side has to be taller than the depth of the box. It will act as a lid with a flap. Cut along the lines with scissors (see diagram 1b).

Warning!

Always ask for an adult's help when working with sharp tools.

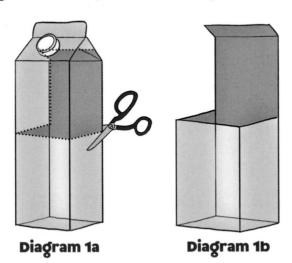

Diagram 1a   **Diagram 1b**

2. Fold down the lid and the flap (see diagram 2a). Draw lines with a permanent marker no more than one inch above and below the fold (see diagram 2b).

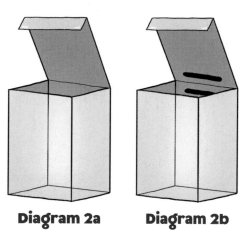

Diagram 2a   **Diagram 2b**

Think about this

Making the lines one inch or less above and below the fold puts more tension on the spring (the plastic strips) when the clown-in-the-box is completed.

3. Holding the plastic bottle, pinch the plastic, and, with scissors, snip a hole in the plastic. Then, cut off the top part of the bottle (see diagram 3).

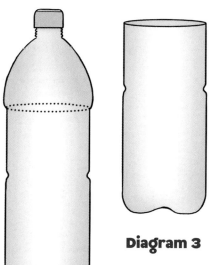

Diagram 3

4. Cut from one end to the other, and then cut the bottom off of the bottle (see diagram 4). Trim the top if it is curved to straighten the edges.

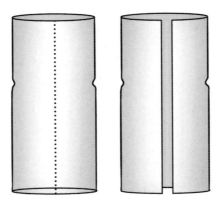

Diagram 4

5. Draw a line 3/4 of an inch from the top of the plastic. Draw a second line 3/4 of an inch below the first (see diagram 5a). Cut the two strips of plastic (see diagram 5b).

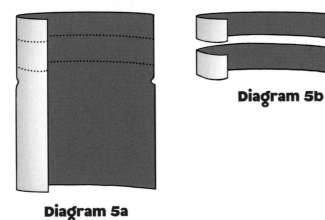

Diagram 5b

Diagram 5a

6. On each strip, draw a line about 1/2 of an inch or more from each end. Then, fold in each end along the line (see diagram 6a) and fold them back out (see diagram 6b).

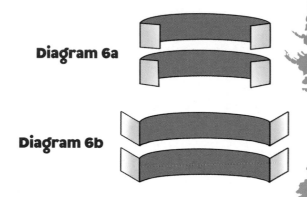

Diagram 6a

Diagram 6b

Think about this!

During the Renaissance, skilled German watchmakers made jack-in-the-boxes as toys for the rich. Turning the crank on the box created music, then the devil or jester would jump out. By the 1930s, the character in the box was a clown and the box was stamped tin, making the toy affordable and available to the masses (Swenson, 2017).

7. Have an adult use an X-Acto or utility knife to carefully make two cuts on the line above the box's fold and two cuts on the line below the fold (see diagram 7).

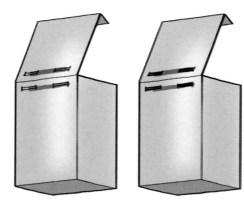

Diagram 7

8. Insert the strips and tape them to the box (see diagram 8). Open and close the lid. If the lid does not bounce open, shorten the strips to add more tension or try a stronger plastic bottle.

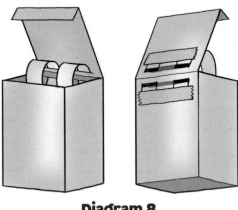

Diagram 8

Think about this!

The plastic strips have material or molecular shape-memory. *Shape-memory* is how metals, polymers, or other materials try to spring or recoil back to their original form—especially if the shape was temperature induced.

9. When the plastic is springy, carefully glue the plastic strips to the box. Tape over the glued plastic (see diagram 9).

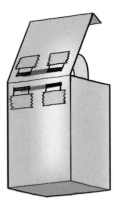

Diagram 9

10. Create a clown or other creature to go inside the box. First, glue a piece of construction paper on the front of the plastic strips (see diagram 10). This will be part of the clown's clothes/body.

Warning!
Put glue on the paper first so that the plastic doesn't melt.

Diagram 10

11. Create a head and arms for your clown on a separate sheet of construction paper. Attach them to the body (see diagram 11).

12. You can make a latch for the box. Using a single hole punch, care-fully punch a hole in the flap. Close the lid, leaving the flap over the front edge, and color in the hole, marking the spot. Punch a hole on your mark in the top edge of the front of the box, then stick a brass fastener (or piece of cardboard) in the punched hole(s).

Troubleshoot This!

✓ Do the clown's hands stick out too far? Fold them a little.
✓ Is the clown not bouncing back up? If the spring is springy enough, then paper or plastic is catching somewhere on the box.

Experiment With This!

✓ Redesign this project. What if the box was a bigger or different shape? What other materials can you use? You could build a larger version and have a ghost or vampire pop out at Halloween. Use the chart on the following page to record how well alternate mate-rials work.

Alternative Materials Record

Original Material	Alternative Material Used	Outcome

Climbing Creature

Supplies

- ❑ Wire hanger
- ❑ Two 6-foot pieces of yarn
- ❑ Cereal box (or similar type of cardboard)
- ❑ Masking tape
- ❑ Decorations (construction paper, paint, etc.)

Tools

- ❑ Adult-size craft scissors
- ❑ Marker
- ❑ Low-temperature mini-glue gun and glue sticks
- ❑ Ruler
- ❑ Single hole punch

What Should Happen

You will cut cereal box cardboard to look like a bug, mouse, rat, cat, bird, or other creature. Then, you will punch holes on each side, decorate it, and sew through each hole with yarn. You will attach the creature to a clothes hanger and hang it on a door. You will pull one side and then the other. It will walk down the door!

INSTRUCTIONS

1. Cut open the cereal box so the cardboard is laid out in a single layer. Then, draw the shape of the creature you intend to create (see diagram 1a). Make the body as square as possible, and cut it out (see diagram 1b). The body has to be big enough to fit four or more holes on each side, along with an arm or leg on each corner, and a head or tail on the ends. If the cardboard is too big, it may become too heavy, and it will not stay in place but will slide down the yarn. Remember the arms, legs, head, and tail add extra weight to your design.

2. Using the single hole punch, punch 4–6 holes down each side of the creature (see diagram 2).

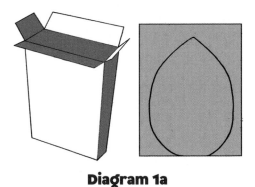

Diagram 1a

Diagram 1b

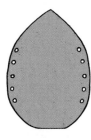

Diagram 2

3. With construction paper or cereal box cardboard, create legs, ears, a tail, a nose, etc., for your creature. Glue the body parts onto the body, and let the glue dry (see diagram 3).

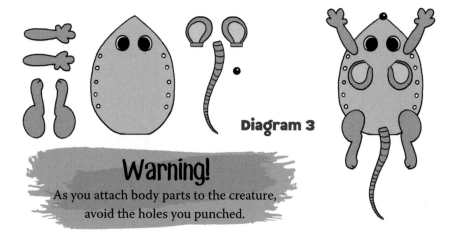

Diagram 3

Warning!
As you attach body parts to the creature, avoid the holes you punched.

4. Weave a 6-foot piece of yarn down each side of the creature. Tie them together at the bottom (the end that the creature is facing) so that the creature does not slip off the yarn (see diagram 4).

Diagram 4

Think about this!
How can you cover the clothes hanger to disguise it?

5. Tie the loose ends of the yarn to the wire hanger (about the width of your creature). Tape the yarn in place (see diagram 5).

6. Hang the wire hanger on the top of a door. Move the creature to the top by pulling the pieces of yarn apart (see diagram 6a). To make it crawl down the yarn, pull one side and then the other (see diagram 6b).

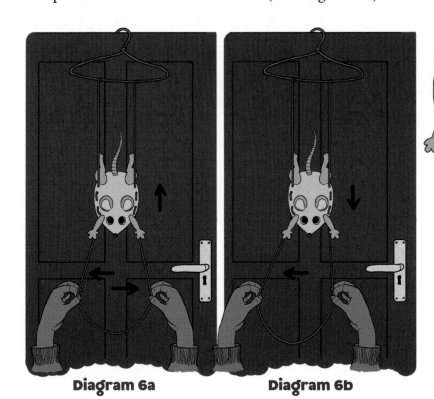

Diagram 5

Diagram 6a   **Diagram 6b**

Troubleshoot This!

✓ If the creature slides down too easily, you need to punch more holes into the side of your creature or use a thicker yarn.

Think about this!

Why does the creature move down the yarn? When you pull one piece of the yarn and the clothes hanger wobbles down, it pulls the creature down the other piece of yarn.

Experiment With This!

✓ Can you design this project so that the creature moves the other direction? Rather than using a wire hanger, try attaching each loose end of the yarn to stationary hooks or screws.

Think about this!

On a stationary hook, when you pull the yarn down, it operates like elastic and stretches through the holes. When you release the yarn and it goes back to its original shape, it pulls the creature up the yarn.

Bobbing Dog

Supplies

- ❑ 3–5 in. plastic container
- ❑ Cereal box (or similar type of cardboard)
- ❑ Decorations (paint, googly eyes, construction paper, markers, etc.)

Tools

- ❑ Adult-size craft scissors
- ❑ Low-temperature mini-glue gun and glue sticks or white glue
- ❑ Permanent marker
- ❑ Pencil

What Should Happen

Using a plastic cup for a body, you will cut notches and attach a strip of cereal box cardboard as the fulcrum glued into the container. Then, you will glue the center of a longer piece of cardboard—the creature's body—to the other end. The head and tail will bob up and down!

Think about this!

This project will expand your knowledge of weights and balances. Keep in mind that a *lever* is a simple machine that helps you lift objects. A *fulcrum* is the pivot point a lever rests on or against.

Think about this!

The bobbing dog will work like a playground seesaw, where a lever rests on a pivot/fulcrum. You will balance both ends so that neither is heavier than the other. The fulcrum is in the middle of the weight, balancing each end.

INSTRUCTIONS

1. Cut the cereal box along the folds to flatten it (see diagram 1a). Cut out a rectangle that is at least twice as long as your plastic container (see diagram 1b). The rectangle's length can be longer than two containers, but its width should be less than one half of the diameter of your container.

Diagram 1a

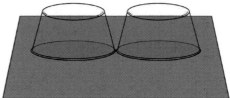

Diagram 1b

2. Draw the creature's head, body, and tail as one piece on the cardboard (see diagram 2a). The tail will act as your counterweight: It should be long enough and heavy enough to balance a lightly decorated head. Cut out the body (see diagram 2b).

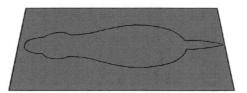

Diagram 2a

Diagram 2b

Think about this!

What can you make besides a dog? How about creating a cat, turtle, rabbit, or even a fish or a snake looking out of a hole?

3. With a marker, draw a line 1/2–2/3 from the bottom of the upside down container. It should be slightly wider than your cardboard creature's body (see diagram 3a). Continue drawing lines to the edge of the cup (see diagram 3b). They can be straight or flared slightly. Repeat on the opposite side of the container (see diagram 3c).

Diagram 3a   **Diagram 3b**   **Diagram 3c**

4. Cut along your lines (see diagram 4).

5. Decorate your creature's body with markers, construction paper, or paint (see diagram 5a). Allow time to dry. Create feet and ears using construction paper or cereal box cardboard (see diagram 5b). You should attach the ears to the body now, but note that the feet will be attached to the plastic container.

 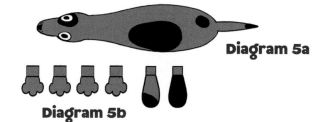

Diagram 5a

Diagram 4

Diagram 5b

6. Find the center of gravity of your creature's body (see diagram 6). Balance the cardboard on your finger. Keep moving your finger until you can let go of the body with your other hand and the creature balances like a seesaw. With a marker or pencil, mark the pivot point.

PIVOT POINT

Diagram 6

> ## Think about this!
>
> Is the pivot point in the center of your creature? Or, is it closer to the head or the tail? Why would it be off center?

7. Cut a 1/2-inch-wide strip of cereal box cardboard. It should be as long as the height of your plastic container. Fold each end by about 1/2 of an inch (see diagram 7).

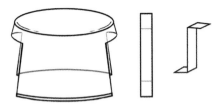

Diagram 7

8. Put glue one end of the folded cardboard strip. Press it inside the center of the plastic container (see diagram 8).

9. Add glue to the other end of the folded cardboard strip. Attach it to the top of the creature at its pivot point. Glue the feet to your container (see diagram 9).

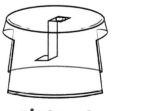

Diagram 8

Diagram 9

10. Paint and decorate your container (see diagram 10).

Diagram 10

Troubleshoot This!

✓ The creature is a seesaw; each end should be balanced as needed.
✓ The pivot may be too long, too short, too wide, or too skinny.

Experiment With This!

✓ Experiment with ideas. What about making the bobbing dog bigger or a different shape? Why will the alternate material(s) work? Why not? Record your results on the chart below.
✓ How could this machine be used in designing new energy or an alternative energy source?

Alternative Materials Record

Original Material	Alternative Material Used	Outcome

Another Bobbing Dog?

Here's another way that you can build the bobbing dog! What are the differences and similarities between the end products? As an engineer, there are always different choices we make when designing. These two projects are the same in that a lever teeters back and forth from a single point. The differences are in the amount of teetering in the one with the craft stick hanging from a string versus the stability of the cardboard bobbing dog hanging from the strip of cardboard.

Supplies

- ❏ Paper egg carton cup
- ❏ Cereal box (or similar type of cardboard)
- ❏ Craft stick
- ❏ Small rock or large bead
- ❏ Marker or pencil
- ❏ String
- ❏ Pipe cleaner
- ❏ Decorations (paint, googly eyes, construction paper, etc.)

Tools

- ❏ Adult-size craft scissors
- ❏ Diagonal cutting pliers
- ❏ Low-temperature mini-glue gun and glue sticks
- ❏ Pencil

What Should Happen

You will use an egg carton cup for the body. You will then attach a string around a decorated craft stick (the head) balanced with a counter-weight and connect the string to the egg carton cup. The head will bob up and down.

INSTRUCTIONS

1. Cut an arch in each side of an egg carton cup (see diagram 1). One should be cut slightly higher for the dog's head.

2. With diagonal cutting pliers, cut the craft stick in half. Decorate the round end of the craft stick to look like a dog (see diagram 2).

Diagram 1   **Diagram 2**

3. Glue the small rock or bead to the other end of the craft stick (see diagram 3). The rock is your counterweight.

4. Find the center of gravity of the craft stick. Balance the stick on your finger. With a marker or a pencil, mark the pivot point. Then, use a small amount of glue on the pivot point and wrap string around the stick at the pivot point (see diagram 4).

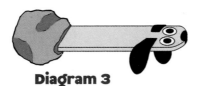 

Diagram 3   **Diagram 4**

5. After the glue dries, hold the end of the string to make sure the head and rock are still balanced (see diagram 5). If not, add glue to either end of the craft stick to balance.

6. Twist a loop in the end of a pipe cleaner and thread the string through the loop (see diagram 6).

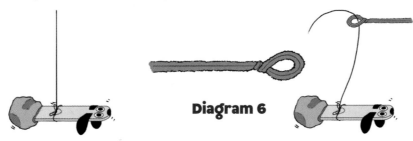

Diagram 6

Diagram 5

7. With a pencil, punch a small hole in the top of the egg carton cup (see diagram 7a). Thread the pipe cleaner up through the hole in the egg carton cup (see diagram 7b). Pull the string through until the dog's head is under the neck hole (the highest arch).

Diagram 7

8. Glue the string to the outside top of the carton cup; cut off the extra (see diagram 8).

9. Decorate the egg carton cup to look like a dog. Add feet and a tail (see diagram 9). Set it in your hand and watch the head bob up and down.

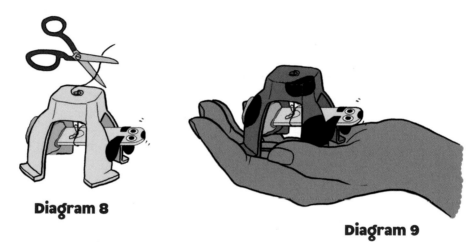

Diagram 8

Diagram 9

Rubber Band-Propelled Car

Supplies

- ❑ Strong 2-liter bottle (leave the label on the soda bottle so you will have a guideline)
- ❑ 1/4-inch dowel (or two chopsticks)
- ❑ Masking tape
- ❑ Four plastic lids of the same size (or two pairs: two smaller lids and two larger lids)
- ❑ 3–6 size #16 or #18 rubber bands
- ❑ Decorations (construction paper, pipe cleaners, etc.)

Tools

- ❑ Adult-size craft scissors
- ❑ Needle nose pliers
- ❑ Low-temperature mini-glue gun and glue sticks
- ❑ Ruler
- ❑ Utility knife
- ❑ Diagonal cutting pliers
- ❑ Nail
- ❑ Sharpened pencil

What Should Happen

You will use a large plastic bottle as the car chassis (its framework) and two dowels as the front and rear axles. You will attach them with hot glue to the four plastic lids, the wheels. The axles will spin in the holes in the bottle, easily and without restriction. Then, you will attach rubber bands to the back axle, pull the rubber bands through the bottle opening, and wrap one around the mouth of the bottle. Roll the car backward to wind it up; let go and the rubber band-propelled car will zoom across the floor!

Think about this!

When building a rubber band car out of a bottle or preparing for any project, you need to explore the *structural integrity* of the materials. Structural integrity is the strength of the materials. Will they last and maintain their strength over the length of time needed?

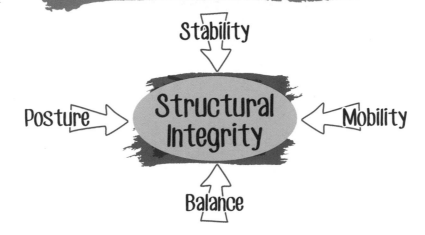

INSTRUCTIONS

1. Fill the bottle about one fourth of the way with tap water. Tighten the cap, and dry off the bottle (see diagram 1).

2. Lay the bottle on its side. Let the water settle and become level (see diagram 2). You can wedge tape or cardboard up against each side of the bottle to hold it still. You're going to use the water as a level to mark the places for your wheels.

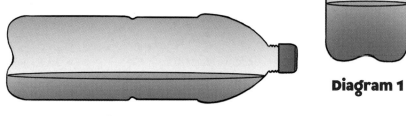

Diagram 1

Diagram 2

3. Use the permanent marker to put a dot where the ridge at the top of the bottle crosses the water level and where the bottom of the label crosses the water level (see diagram 3 on the following page). Either turn the bottle around and let the water settle again, or walk around to the other side of the table. Mark the same points on the other side of the bottle. Empty the water, and remove the cap and the label.

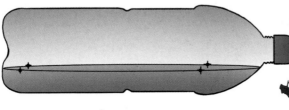

Diagram 3

Think about this!

Look at the dots. Do they all look even? Are they the same horizontally and vertically? If the dots do not match, then what could happen to the wheels? Will the wheels touch the ground? Will the car turn instead of driving straight?

4. Draw a large rectangle about 1/2 of an inch just inside the dots (see diagram 4a). This will be the bottom of the car. Have an adult poke a hole in the middle of the rectangle with the utility knife or the X-Acto blade (a nice big X so you can fit the scissors into the slit). Then, cut along your marker line. Or, if you are using a weaker plastic bottle, cut two small rectangles in the bottle in line with your dots (see diagram 4b). The rectangles need to be large enough for you to fit your fingers and a single hole punch.

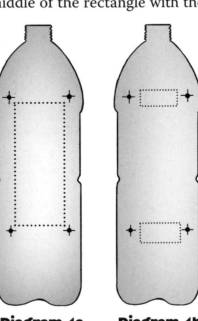

Diagram 4a   **Diagram 4b**

5. Use the hole punch and punch holes through the dots you made (see diagram 5a). To insert a 1/4-inch dowel, you may need to gently twist a pair of scissors or needle nose pliers into the holes to make them large enough for the dowel to spin easily (see diagram 5b). You just finished the hardest part!

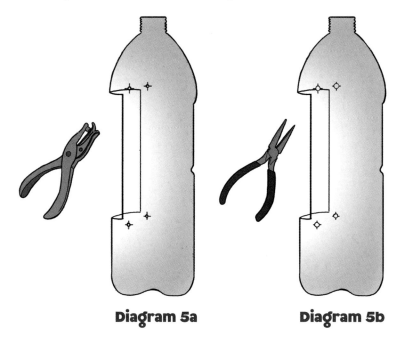

Diagram 5a   **Diagram 5b**

6. The dowels will act as your axles. Insert the dowels through the holes on the bottle. Then, using the permanent marker, mark the dowels so that at least 1 1/2 inches of axle protrudes on each side (they can be longer; see diagram 6). Cut away the excess with diagonal cutting pliers as needed.

Diagram 6

7. Poke a hole in the center of each lid by carefully pushing a nail through the soft plastic. Then, insert a sharpened pencil to make the holes bigger (see diagram 7). Be careful not to tear the lids.

Diagram 7

8. Slide each lid onto a dowel *but not against the car*. Then, glue each wheel to the dowel (see diagram 8 on the following page). It's important to take your time so that the wheels are straight, but don't over glue, because you may need to remove a wheel later.

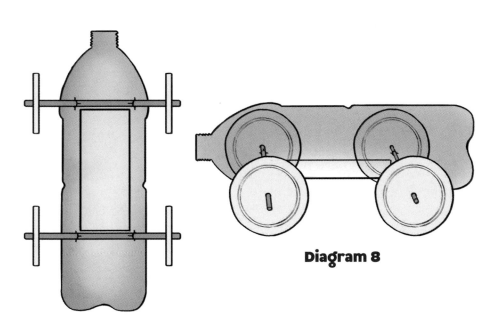

Diagram 8

9. Connect 3–6 rubber bands. Put one rubber band through another and then put one end of the first rubber band through its other end (see diagram 9a). Pull tight and repeat for each rubber band. The chain of rubber bands should be long enough to extend from the back axle (at the bottom of the bottle) to the mouth of the bottle (see diagram 9b).

Diagram 9a

Diagram 9b

10. Put one end of the rubber band chain under the back axle and slip the other end of the chain through it (see diagram 10). Pull it tight.

11. Threading the rubber band chain through the bottle, take the loose end of the rubber band chain and push it out of the top of the bottle. Loop it around the top (as you would tie hair in a ponytail; see diagram 11). Do not put the bottle cap back on. It will cut your rubber bands.

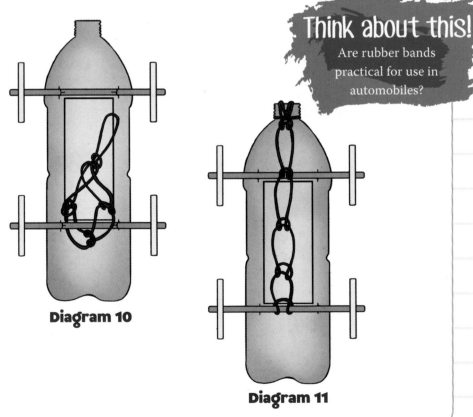

Diagram 10

Diagram 11

Think about this!

Are rubber bands practical for use in automobiles?

12. Stick tape across the rubber band on the back axle (see diagram 12). This will keep the rubber band from slipping.

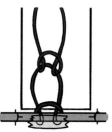

Diagram 12

Warning!

Do not glue the rubber band because you will need to replace your rubber bands someday. Also, hot glue will damage the integrity of the rubber band.

13. Roll the car backward to wind it up (see diagram 13). Let it go! Then, try using your hand to turn the back wheel to wind up the car. Set it down, and let it go. Now, wind it even tighter. Let it go. What's the best way to wind up the car?

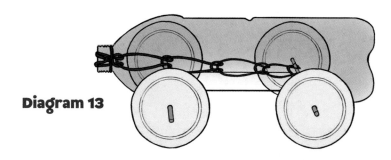

Diagram 13

Think about this!

The rubber band-propelled car's cost to the environment is minimal because it is mostly made out of recyclable trash. What else can be done to make this car design more ecologically efficient? Can this design be used in the real world?

14. Decorate your car. Make passengers out of construction paper or other materials. Create seats for them and attach them to the vehicle (see diagram 14).

Diagram 14

Warning!

Do not put hot glue directly onto the plastic bottle. The plastic will melt. When decorating, squeeze the glue on the paper (or other material), let it cool for a second, and then place on the plastic bottle.

Troubleshoot This!

- ✓ If the holes in the bottle are uneven, then put a larger lid/wheel on the side that is not able to reach the ground.
- ✓ Check for stray hot glue strings.
- ✓ Is the rubber band hitting against the front axle? Remove the rubber band from the end of the bottle, pull the rubber band chain to the other side of the axle, stretch it, and refasten the rubber band to the end of the bottle by twisting it around the threads.
- ✓ Sometimes the car just needs more weight so it will have better traction. You can add decorations above the rear wheels to improve traction. Keep in mind that too much weight will cause drag and slow down the car!
- ✓ Are the axles sliding around and causing wheels to hit against each other or the chassis? Create separators by cutting four 1-inch squares of cardboard. Punch holes in the middle of each square and cut slits to attach the separators between the wheel and the bottle (see diagram 15).

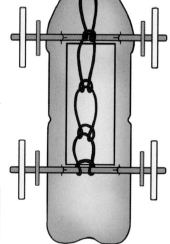

Diagram 15

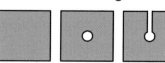

Experiment With This!

✓ Do you want your car to go farther? Or faster? There are many ways you can change your car design. Remember to record your results on the Test Drive Record on page 81!

» What happens if you use bigger wheels?

» What if you use bigger wheels in the back and smaller wheels in the front (see diagram 16)?

» What about a car with CDs for wheels?

» Does the weight of your car affect how it travels? Try adding extra weight over the front wheels for traction, then the back wheels. Which works better?

✓ Can you think of a way to motorize this car?

✓ Do your wheels spin or slip on the ground? What can you add to make them grip better?

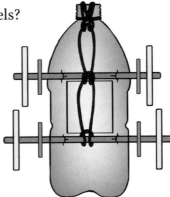

Diagram 16

Test Drive Record

Distance	Time	Velocity

Catapult

Supplies

- ❑ 12–14 in. x 8–10 in. corrugated cardboard or foam core
- ❑ Two toilet paper tubes
- ❑ Masking tape
- ❑ 1/4-inch dowel 8–10 inches long
- ❑ Paint stick or wooden ruler
- ❑ Pipe cleaner
- ❑ Two craft sticks
- ❑ Size #18 or larger rubber band
- ❑ Small plastic container or paper cup
- ❑ Decorations (paint, construction paper, etc.)
- ❑ Safe projectiles (marshmallows, egg carton cups, bottle caps, small drinking cups)

Tools

- ❑ Adult-size craft scissors
- ❑ Low-temperature mini-glue gun and glue sticks
- ❑ Single hole punch
- ❑ Diagonal cutting pliers
- ❑ Marker or pencil
- ❑ Paintbrush

What Should Happen

You will mount two posts on a cardboard platform and insert a dowel from post to post. Then, you will attach a lever across a fulcrum. You will attach a rubber band that will allow the lever to snap with enough force to send a projectile through the air.

Think about this!

A catapult is a mechanical device that shoots or launches a projectile by releasing stored energy. Catapults were ancient and medieval artillery, along with early machines such as the ballista, mangonel, and trebuchet. The mangonel and ballista were similar to crossbows, shooting huge projectiles, whereas the trebuchet used counterweights to fling the objects.

The catapult was used to hurl fire, oil, animals, and other objects over a great distance or height. Using force and friction, the basics of physics, and not an explosive catalyst, catapults could fling objects over castle walls or across moats.

INSTRUCTIONS

1. Glue down the toilet paper tubes upright in the center of the cardboard rectangle. They need to be about 3–6 inches apart, depending on the size of your paint stick/lever. Tape the tubes to the base, and then tape down your tape (see diagram 1).

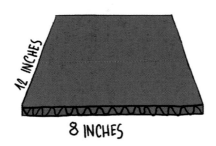

12 INCHES

8 INCHES

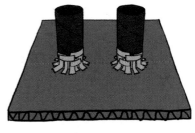

Diagram 1

2. Place a single hole punch as far down the side of a toilet paper tube as it will go. Punch a 1/4-inch hole into each side of the tube (see diagram 2a). Do the same to the second tube. Push the 1/4-inch dowel through both tubes with an inch or more extending on each side (see diagram 2b). The dowel will be a fulcrum that supports the catapult's lever.

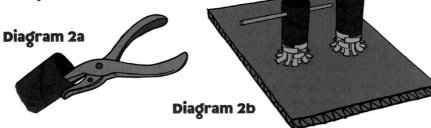

Diagram 2a

Diagram 2b

3. Cut a craft stick in half using the diagonal cutting pliers. To stabilize the lever, glue half of the craft stick on each end of the wooden ruler (see diagram 3). This will provide structural balance.

4. Lean the wooden ruler against the dowel and tie them together with a pipe cleaner. The catapult will be more stable if you tie them together in an X-pattern (see diagram 4):
   » Lay the pipe cleaner diagonally across the lever. Pull both ends tightly around the back, behind the lever and fulcrum. Tightly twist the two ends together.
   » Pull both ends of the pipe cleaner around to the front on the two open corners. Tightly twist the two ends together.

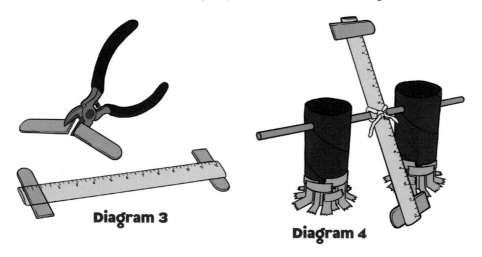

Diagram 3

Diagram 4

5. Use a pencil to carefully poke a hole through the cardboard base (see diagram 5a). Loop one end of the rubber band around the end of the lever. Squeeze the other end of the rubber band, and push it through the hole (see diagram 5b).

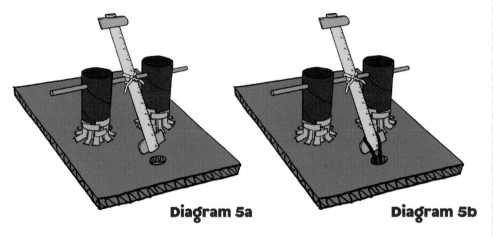

Diagram 5a   **Diagram 5b**

6. Cut a craft stick in half using the diagonal cutting pliers (save one half for another project). On the underside of the cardboard base, wrap the end of the rubber band around half of the craft stick. Then, tape the craft stick to the cardboard (see diagram 6).

Diagram 6

Warning!

Do not use hot glue to attach the craft stick to the cardboard. Using tape, you will be able to easily replace your rubber band if it breaks.

7. Glue and tape a small plastic container (or paper cup) to the other end of the lever (see diagram 7).

Diagram 7

8. Create safe projectiles to catapult (see diagram 8a):

» Glue together egg carton cups (or mini water cups) to make creatures. Decorate with paint, markers, glue, and/or paper (see diagram 8b).

» Decorate marshmallows and bottle caps with paint, markers, glue, etc., to make small creatures (see diagram 8c).

Diagram 8a

Diagram 8b

Diagram 8c

9. Place an egg carton or marshmallow creature in the container (see diagram 9). Push down the end of the lever that holds the container, and let the catapult go! Test different projectiles, and record your results.

Diagram 9

Warning!

Do not aim the catapult at anyone or anything. Always use safe, harmless projectiles.

Think about this!

A catapult flings an object through the air using counterweights, tension, or torque. What contemporary materials could you use if you were designing a full-sized catapult?

Think about this!

Early writings indicate catapults were already around during the 3rd and 4th centuries BC. Catapults were also used during World War I. But you can find modern catapults on aircraft carriers. The distance needed to lift an airplane can be too great for aircraft carrier, as there is not enough room for a standard runway. A slingshot catapult is used to launch the aircraft. What else can catapults be used for in modern life?

Troubleshoot This!

✓ If the egg carton characters do not fly out of the cup, then the cup is either too tall or too skinny. Try larger containers.

Experiment With This!

✓ Slide the wooden ruler up or down the fulcrum to change the angle between the lever and the base. See if larger angles increase or decrease the firing range of your catapult. The change in angle will also change the height at which the object flies. If you were trying to get an object over a castle wall, what would be more important: the height or the distance an object will fly?

✓ Build a quick and easy catapult. Use a flexible plastic spoon and a plastic bottle, such as a vitamin bottle. Remove the lid. Glue and then tape the bottle on its side to a corrugated cardboard base. Glue and then tape the spoon upright against the pill bottle, handle against the base. Lay the lid against the spoon handle on the base. Glue and then tape the lid against the handle to keep the spoon in place. Place an egg-carton character in the spoon top, then pull back gently and release.

✓ Build a counterweight trebuchet. Follow Steps 1–4. Then, wrap duct tape around a rock and one end of the lever. Follow Steps 7 and 8. Then, lift the rock off of the base, place something in the plastic container, and then release the rock (the rock should thud against the base; see diagram 10). Catapult lightweight objects across the room.

Diagram 10

Think about this!

A trebuchet has a counterweight on one end and a slingshot on the other. The counterweight has to be heavier than the flung object. You can slide the lever across the fulcrum, making the distance between the rock and the fulcrum shorter or longer. What does that do to the height and distance of projectiles as you release them?

Pivot

Counterweight

Throwing Arm

Frame

It Lays an Egg

Supplies

- ❑ 1-gallon jug
- ❑ 4- to 5-inch plastic lid
- ❑ Four size #16 or #18 rubber bands
- ❑ Two craft sticks
- ❑ Masking tape
- ❑ 2- to 5-inch Styrofoam ball or lightweight plastic cup
- ❑ 18-inch square piece of corrugated cardboard

- ❑ Two toilet paper tubes
- ❑ Decorations (paint, construction paper, eyes, feathers, etc., for body parts)
- ❑ Plastic eggs

Think about this!

Explore the structural integrity of your materials. To use fewer resources, manufacturers have thinned out the walls of most bottles, saving on plastic and other material. So, pick your gallon jug, toilet paper tubes, and cardboard with that in mind.

Tools

- ❑ Adult-size craft scissors
- ❑ Utility knife
- ❑ Single hole punch
- ❑ Diagonal cutting pliers
- ❑ Permanent marker and pencil
- ❑ Low-temperature mini-glue gun and glue sticks

- ❑ Plastic lid for tracing (smaller than the 4- to 5-inch lid in supplies)
- ❑ Bottle cap for tracing (larger than the diameter of the eggs; optional)

What Should Happen

Using a water or milk jug, you will add rubber bands, plastic lids, cardboard tube legs, and corrugated cardboard feet to create a creature, such as a duck, with a hole on top of it and underneath it. Then, you will drop a plastic egg through the hole on top of the duck's back, and push the body down, causing the rubber bands to stretch. The egg will drop out of the bottom!

Think about this!
What other egg-laying creatures can you make? Some mammals, like the platypus, and amphibians, like frogs, lay eggs. Some dinosaurs laid eggs. And don't forget about mythical creatures like dragons or movie creatures like Godzilla!

INSTRUCTIONS

1. On the side of the jug by the handle, draw or trace a 2-inch diameter circle in the middle of the flat area (see diagram 1). Then, have an adult use a utility knife to cut an X in the middle of the circle so you can cut it out. This side will be the top of the duck, where you insert the egg.

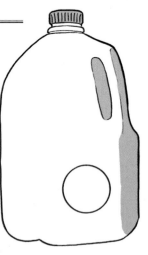

Diagram 1

2. On the opposite side of the jug, trace the smaller plastic lid (see Tools list; diagram 2). Have an adult use a utility knife to cut an X in the middle of the circle so you can cut it out. This side will be the bottom of the jug.

Think about this!

Your creature is a seesaw. The weight of the head has to be countered by the weight of the tail. So, it is probably a good idea, depending on the creature you have chosen and the amount of decorations, to put the large circle (the underbelly), as close to the head as possible.

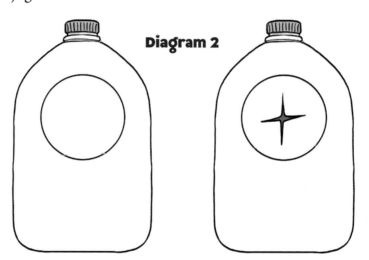

Diagram 2

3. Push the hole punch as far as it will go over the edges of the hole, and punch four holes in the plastic jug—one on each side (see diagram 3).

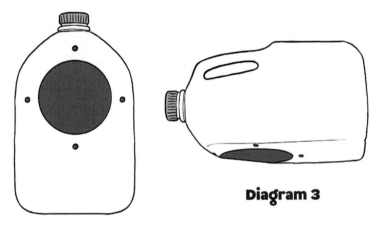

Diagram 3

4. For a chicken or other bird-like creature, glue the polystyrene ball to the mouth of the jug (see diagram 4a). Draw a beak on cardboard or construction paper. Cut it out, then fold it and attach it to the head (see diagram 4b). Add other features (eyes, etc.). Paint the jug and set it aside to dry.

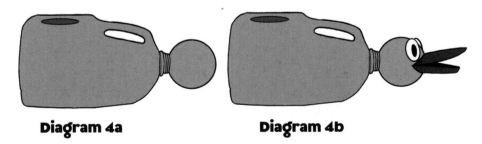

Diagram 4a **Diagram 4b**

Think about this!

You could use a small paper cup or other material for the head, depending on what your creature is going to be and the shape of its head. Do not make the head heavier than the tail of your animal as you decorate. A too-heavy head will cause it to tip forward.

As you paint the jug, use a flexible paint that will stick to it: acrylic paint or tempera paint mixed with tacky glue or a drop of dish soap.

5. Draw a giant heart on the 18-inch piece of cardboard (see diagram 5a). Use this as a template to create feet for your duck (see diagram 5b).

Diagram 5a   **Diagram 5b**

6. Cut the two toilet paper tubes length-wise (see diagram 6a). Roll them up thinly enough to look like duck legs (see diagram 6b; if it is difficult to roll the tube, try rolling the tube around a marker). Then, hot glue under the edge and press it together. As needed, trim the ends of the legs so that they are the same length. Wrap masking tape around each one to hold it together and strengthen the legs.

Diagram 6a

Diagram 6b

7. Glue both legs upright and close together in the center of the feet. Add more glue around the edges for support (see diagram 7).

8. Tape the legs to the feet for more structural support (see diagram 8). Tape down your tape.

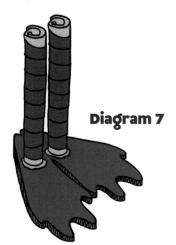

Diagram 7

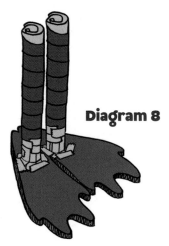

Diagram 8

9. Cut an oval of corrugated cardboard, smaller than your plastic lid but bigger than the legs. Glue the oval to the top of the legs (see diagram 9). Tape the legs to the oval for more structural support. Tape down your tape.

Diagram 9

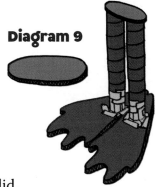

10. Draw a plus sign in the center of the plastic lid. Use a single hole punch to add a hole at the end of each line (see diagram 10).

11. Add glue to the inside of the center of the lid. Stick the legs to the lid using the cardboard oval (see diagram 11).

Diagram 10

12. You will glue around the edge of the oval, securing it to the lid. It's critical that you do a small section at a time, and carefully and immediately add tape (see diagram 12). Consider cutting your tape pieces ahead of time and lining them up at the edge of your workspace. Keep gluing until you work all the way around the oval. Tape down your tape.

Diagram 11   **Diagram 12**

13. Stand the legs upright (see diagram 13). This is a good time to paint the feet and legs. Let them dry.

14. Put a rubber band through each hole in the plastic lid. Then, on each rubber band, insert one loop through the other loop. Pull each rubber band tightly (see diagram 14).

Think about this!

If the rubber bands don't stay connected, put a piece of tape on each rubber band.

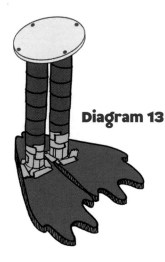

Diagram 13

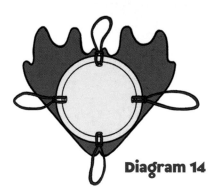

Diagram 14

15. Use the diagonal cutting pliers to cut the craft sticks in half (see diagram 15).

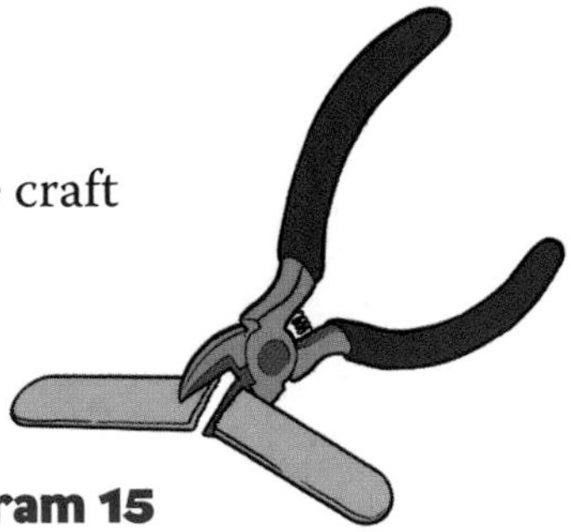

Diagram 15

16. Stick the plastic lid into the bottom of the jug. It is all flexible plastic—just squeeze and push (see diagram 16).

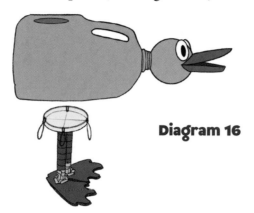

Diagram 16

17. Pull each rubber band through the holes on the jug (see diagram 17a). Put a craft stick through each rubber band and wrap the rubber band around the stick (see diagram 17b). Tape each one down (see diagram 17c).

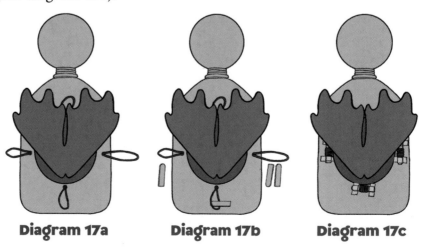

Diagram 17a   **Diagram 17b**   **Diagram 17c**

18. Test your duck: Drop an egg, or eggs, into the jug through the hole at the top. Push the body toward the ground, then let it go (see diagram 18a). When it comes back up, an egg should be at the duck's feet (see diagram 18b)!

19. Add other features, such as feathers and wings to your duck.

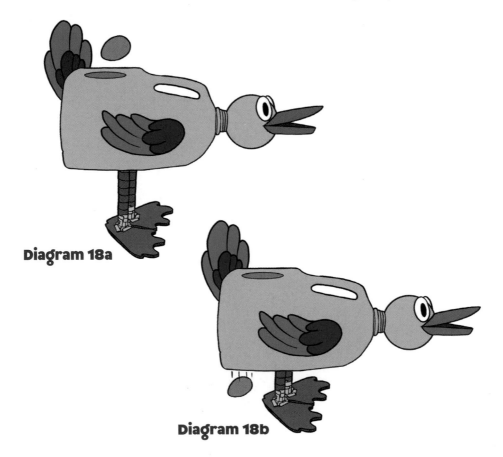

Diagram 18a

Diagram 18b

Troubleshoot This!

✓ If the egg does not come out easily, you may have too much tension in your rubber bands (they may be stretched too tightly to release easily). You may need to unwind the rubber bands that are around the craft stick, or you may need to cut the bottom of the hole of the duck a little bigger.

Experiment With This!

✓ Redesign: What else can you make with this idea? Think about anything removes a plug, allowing something to come through, and then puts the plug back in place, like filling ketchup bottles in a factory over and over again with precise amounts. This process regulates the volume of the liquid being pushed out. Another example is a gumball machine. You put a coin in a slot and turn the handle. This rotates a disk, allowing a gumball to move over the opening. Then, the gumball falls through the hole.

Motorcar

Supplies

- ❑ 4 x 6 in. piece of 1/4-inch thick corrugated cardboard (or foam core)
- ❑ Extra cardboard (to make 4–8 1-inch squares)
- ❑ Marker or pencil
- ❑ 1/4-inch dowel
- ❑ Masking tape
- ❑ Smooth swimming pool noodle (noodles with ridges will cause the tires to drag)
- ❑ Toilet paper tube
- ❑ Two AA batteries
- ❑ Cereal box (or similar type of cardboard)
- ❑ Plastic sport water bottle cap

- ❑ 22-gauge copper wire (two pieces at least 14 inches long each, completely stripped, and at least 24 inches of additional wire, unstripped)
- ❑ 1.5- to 3-volt DC, single-speed motor (see diagram)
- ❑ Push on, push off switch (or two brass fasteners)
- ❑ 7/8- to 1-inch dowel (or a small chunk of wood)
- ❑ Decorations (paint, construction paper, egg carton cups, bottle caps etc.)

Motor & Switch

Think about this!

✓ Corrugated cardboard weighs less than foam core but bends where you may not want it to bend. Foam core is strong and tough, but a little heavy. You want to keep the weight of the car as light as possible.

✓ Most pool noodles have holes in the middle: You will want whatever size dowel you select to fit loosely through your pool noodle.

Tools

- Adult-size craft scissors
- Hacksaw
- Ruler
- Low-temperature mini-glue gun and glue sticks
- Single hole punch
- Needle-nose pliers
- Hammer and nail (smaller in diameter than the motor shaft)
- Wire stripper
- Paintbrush
- Diagonal pliers

What Should Happen

For this three-wheel motorcar, only one wheel will connect to the motor. You will build a battery pack out of a toilet paper tube, connect the motor to the battery pack, and connect the motor and battery pack to a switch. Then, you will switch the car on and watch it go!

INSTRUCTIONS

1. In the center of one short side of the 4 in. x 6 in. rectangle of corrugated cardboard (or foam core), draw and then cut a notch 1 1/2 to 2 inches wide and 3 to 3 1/2 inches long (see diagram 1). The front tire will go into this slot. This becomes your car frame.

Diagram 1

2. With the diagonal cutters or needle-nose pliers, cut a 10-inch length from the 1/4-inch dowel. About 1/2 inch from the end of the car frame opposite the slot, lay the dowel, centered, across the car (see diagram 2a). The dowel is your axle. Securely tape it down using long strips of masking tape (see diagram 2b). Smooth the tape so it stays in place.

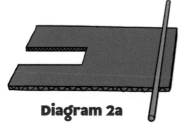

Diagram 2a

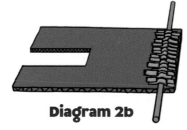

Diagram 2b

3. Tape across the tape (see diagram 3a). Make sure that the axle is secure. Don't glue the dowel to the frame because you may need to adjust it later. Flip the frame over. The top of the car is now facing up (see diagram 3b).

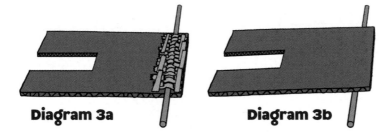

Diagram 3a   **Diagram 3b**

4. Measure your tires. Mark off the noodle in equal 1- to 2-inch increments for the two back tires and no more than 1-inch for the front tire (see diagram 4). The front tire has to fit in the slot in the front of the frame, with lots of room to turn.

5. Keep one hand firmly on the noodle. With an adult's help, use a hacksaw to cut the three wheels from the noodle (see diagram 5).

Diagram 4   **Diagram 5**

6. If the swimming pool noodle does not have a hole in the middle, carefully measure to find the center of each back wheel (see diagram 6). If the hole is not in the center, then the car may not work as well. It's like having the brakes on all of the time. Mark the centers with a marker. Use a 1/4-inch dowel to punch a hole in the middle of each back wheel.

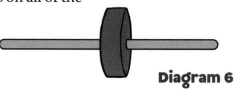

Diagram 6

Think about this!

Some noodles already have holes in the center, but they are larger than the diameter of the dowel. They work easily for the front wheel, but you will need to put hubcaps on them for the back wheels.

✓ Cut four 1-inch squares of cardboard. With the single hole punch, punch a hole into the exact center of each (see diagram a).

✓ Carefully glue around the edge hole in the wheel and place the cardboard over it. Press lightly until the hubcap stays on (see diagram b).

✓ Flip the wheel over and repeat with the other hubcap. Be sure to align the hole in the second hubcap with the hole in the first before you glue it down. If the wheel does not move freely when you put it on the axle, twist a pencil or the tip of the needle-nose pliers around in the holes to loosen them.

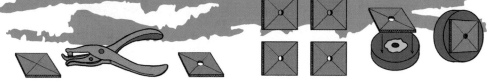

Diagram a   **Diagram b**

7. Cut four 1-inch cardboard squares. With the hole punch, punch a hole in the center of each (see diagram 7a). Place one square on the axle on each side of the frame (see diagram 7b). Do not glue them. These two work as separators so that the wheels do not catch on the frame. Slide the wheels onto the dowel, and then slide on the other two squares. Tape or glue around the hole to keep the two outer squares secure. The wheels should spin easily and have lots of room to move back and forth between the two separators (see diagram 7c). If they do not spin easily, use a dowel or pencil to enlarge the holes in the center of the wheels.

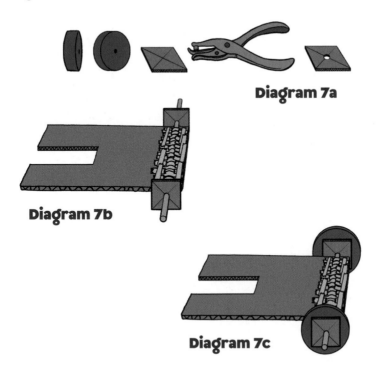

Diagram 7a

Diagram 7b

Diagram 7c

8. Start creating your battery pack. Cut the toilet paper tube lengthwise (see diagram 8a). Cut another lengthwise segment off, 1 1/2 to 2 inches from side (see diagram 8b). Discard the piece.

Diagram 8a

Diagram 8b

9. Roll the toilet paper tube around a marker about the same diameter as the AA batteries (see diagram 9a). Unroll the tube slightly, run some glue along its edge, and then reroll the tube. Remove the marker. Insert one battery to make sure it fits loosely, but not too loosely (see diagram 9b).

Diagram 9a   **Diagram 9b**

10. Cut several strips of masking tape and attach the ends to your worktable to have them ready. Wrap the strips around the toilet paper tube, covering its length to hold it securely (see diagram 10).

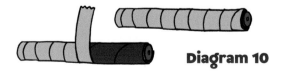

Diagram 10

11. Grab the end of the stripped 14-inch long 22-gauge wire with a pair of needle-nose pliers. Wrap the wire up the tip of the pliers to make a spring (see diagram 11a). Cut the wire about 1 1/2 inches below the spring (see diagram 11b). The wire is thin enough to cut with scissors. Carefully remove the spring from the pliers.

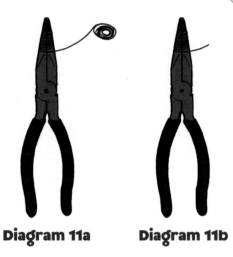

Diagram 11a   **Diagram 11b**

12. On cereal box cardboard, use a marker to trace a circle using one end of the battery pack tube (see diagram 12a), or you can trace a water bottle cap. Cut around the outside of the circle so it is slightly bigger than the end of the battery tube. With the pencil, punch a small hole directly in its center (see diagram 12b).

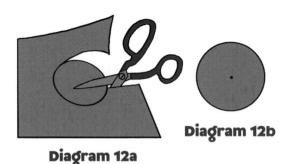

Diagram 12b

Diagram 12a

13. Straighten the stem of the spring (see diagram 13a). Push the straight part of the wire through the hole in the cardboard circle so that the spring rests on the plain side of the cardboard (see diagram 13b).

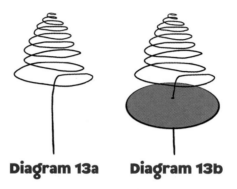

Diagram 13a   **Diagram 13b**

14. Add hot glue on the cardboard under the spring (see diagram 14). Gently tug the straight part of the wire until the bottom of the coil rest in the glue. Glue will also get on a small length of the straight edge, so the spring will be glued inside the hole as well. Peel off any stray glue after it has cooled.

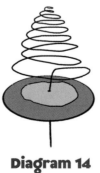

Diagram 14

Warning!

Glue coating the battery pack will keep it from working, so be careful not to get glue on top of the spiral of the spring or too far down on the stem.

15. Trim the end of the toilet paper tube to make it nice and even. Glue the cardboard circle, spring inside, to the rim of the toilet paper tube (see diagram 15a). For added support, add more glue around the outside where the circle and the tube connect. After the glue is dry, insert the batteries with the negative end of one battery touching the positive end of the other (see diagram 15b).

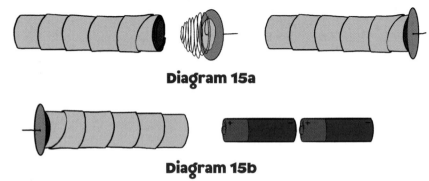

Diagram 15a

Diagram 15b

16. Trim the tube almost to the edge of the batteries (see diagram 16). Don't cut too much off, but cut enough so the copper wire in the cap you are going to make will touch the batteries.

17. Use a nail and hammer to punch a hole in the center top of the plastic cap (see diagram 17). If you use a sports cap, you already have a hole in your cap.

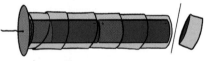

Diagram 16

Diagram 17

18. Make another copper spring as you did in Steps 11 and 13 (see diagram 18a). Insert the straight piece through the hole in the cap from the inside out (see diagram 18b). Glue the bottom of the spring into the cap. Be careful not to get any on top of the spring or on the stem coming out the other end of the cap.

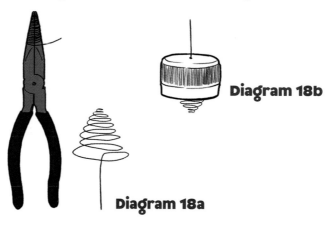

Diagram 18b

Diagram 18a

Think about this!

If you don't have a plastic cap, use the strip of toilet paper tube. Cut a 1-inch strip and glue it into a ring. Cut a circle out of cereal box cardboard slightly larger than the end of the tube. Punch a hole in the center of the circle. Glue the circle to the tube, and then glue the spring into it (see diagram). The ring has to be larger than the battery pack tube.

19. Place the cap on the open end of the battery pack tube (see diagram 19a). If it doesn't fit snugly, remove it and wrap masking tape around the end of the tube (see diagram 19b), replacing the cap frequently, testing it until it fits snugly but comes off easily.

Diagram 19a   **Diagram 19b**

20. **Test it!** Check that your battery pack works: Attach a piece of wire to each motor connector. Touch the end of each wire of your battery pack to each end of the wires attached to the motor.

Think about this!

If the motor doesn't hum and the spindle doesn't spin, check to make sure that you have inserted the batteries with negative touching positive, and that the copper springs are touching the batteries.

21. Using a small amount of hot glue, attach the battery pack right in front of the axle. Do not glue down the battery pack's cap. Tape the battery pack securely in front of and parallel to the axle with masking tape (see diagram 21). Do not put tape on the cap. Tape down your tape.

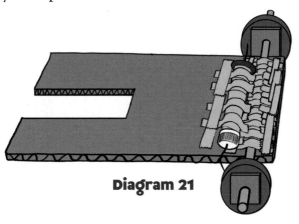

Diagram 21

22. Add your switch. Punch a hole on one side of the front of the car the size of the switch (see diagram 22). Remove the nut from the switch. Insert the switch into the hole, and then screw the nut back on. Leave the washer off if the cardboard is too thick.

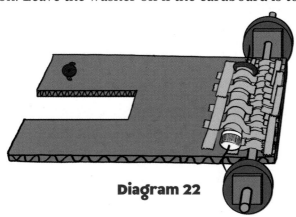

Diagram 22

23. Saw a 1/2- to 3/4-inch piece from the 7/8- to 1-inch dowel. Use a hammer and nail or ask an adult to use a drill with a 1/32 bit to drill a hole through the center of the dowel piece (see diagram 23a). Push the rod on the motor into the hole in the dowel, leaving a small gap between the wood and the motor (see diagram 23b).

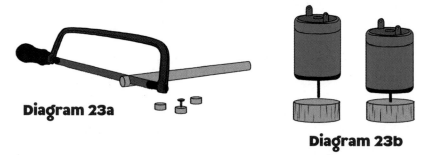

Diagram 23a

Diagram 23b

Think about this!

Any small piece of scrap wood will work just as well as the dowel. Dowels are made of hard wood and can crack easily. Keep in mind that if the hole in the dowel is too loose, the dowel will fly off the motor when it is turned on. If the dowel does fly off, replace it with a new piece of wood.

24. Using a marker and the dowel piece, trace a circle onto the immediate center of the front tire (the pool noodle you cut and set aside earlier). Cut the circle out of the wheel, being careful not to cut it too big (see diagram 24a). Run some glue around the inside of the hole, and insert the dowel piece (see diagram 24b). If the noodle already has a large center hole, then just glue the dowel piece inside.

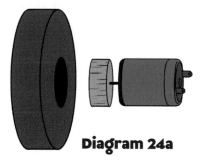

Diagram 24a

Diagram 24b

25. Cut strips of masking tape long enough to go over the motor and attach to the bottom of the car on each side. Place the strips on the edge of your worktable, ready to use. Put one piece of tape on the motor. Squirt a little hot glue then set the motor on the opposite side from the switch at the front of the car, with the wheel inserted into the notch, not touching any cardboard (see diagram 25). Smooth your tape down right up against the motor so the motor does not wiggle. Secure with several more pieces of tape.
Tape down your tape.

Think about this!

Make sure the wheel isn't touching anything. Friction will cause the motor to slow down or stop completely.

Diagram 25

26. Measure the distances between the battery pack and the switch, the switch and the motor, and the motor and the battery pack. Add at least 2 inches to each measurement. Cut one piece of 22-gauge coated electrical wire for each measurement (see diagram 26). With the wire stripper, strip the ends of each wire 3/4 to 1 inch at each end.

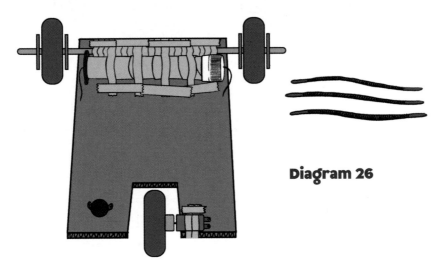

Diagram 26

27. Tightly twist together one stripped end of the battery pack-to-switch wire with the wire extending from the cardboard circle of the battery pack. Insert the other stripped end into the hole on one prong of the switch; twist tightly (see diagram 27).

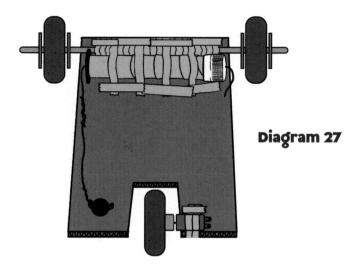

Diagram 27

Think about this!

It is best to stick the wire through the hole in the post on the switch and motor, wrap the wire around the post, and then twist it together (see diagram a). However, you may find it easier to slip it through the hole in the post, and then twist it tightly together (see diagram b).

Diagram a

Diagram b

28. Tightly twist together one stripped end of the battery pack-to-motor wire with the wire extending from the plastic cap on the battery pack. Insert the other stripped end through the hole on one prong of the motor (see diagram 28).

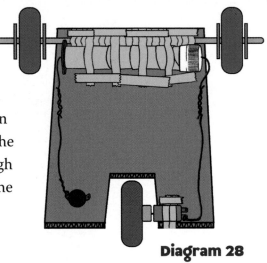

Diagram 28

29. Insert one stripped end of the remaining wire through the hole on the other prong on the switch. Twist tightly. Then insert the other end through the hole on the other prong of the motor (see diagram 29). Twist tightly.

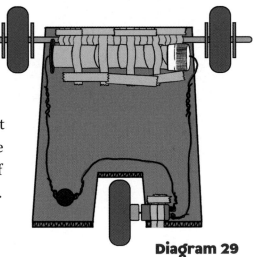

Diagram 29

30. Securely tape all covered wires down (see diagram 30). Be careful that the wires do not touch the wheel. Tape down your tape.

Warning!
Do not put the wheels up against anyone's face or hair.

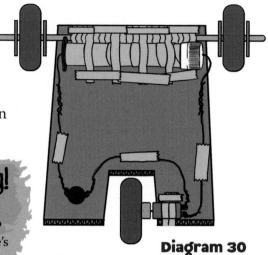

Diagram 30

31. Turn your car over and push the switch. If the car goes backward, take the batteries out and reverse them, being careful to keep positive to negative end. The spindle on the motor will turn in either direction.

32. Paint and decorate your car. You can even add lightweight eggcarton seats (see diagram 32).

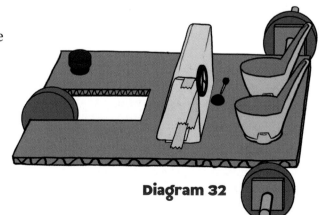

Diagram 32

Troubleshoot This!

- ✓ If the car is not running, you may need to push the battery pack cap more snugly onto the tube; it may have come loose.
- ✓ Squeeze the connections to make sure everything is touching.
- ✓ How can you make sure your batteries are good? Disconnect your motor from the switch and the battery pack. Lay one battery on the table. Touch each end with the wires connected to the motor. If the motor spins, the battery is good. Check the other battery in the same way.

Experiment With This!

- ✓ What other materials can you use to create the motorcar? Why will the alternate material(s) work? Why not?
- ✓ Make two cars, one with a foam core base and the other with a corrugated cardboard base. Race them to record which is faster most often. Speculate on the reasons for the results.
- ✓ Can you use something besides a switch in your wiring? Try brass fasteners! Follow Steps 1–21, and then punch two holes in the front side of the car, and insert two brass fasteners. Follow the steps for wiring your motorcar, treating the brass fasteners like the two holes on the switch. Then, to make the circuit complete, you will need to connect the two brass fasteners with copper wire.

Wrap one stripped end of the wire around a fastener and make a hook with the other end. Slide the hook under the other brass fastener to turn your car on. Slide it out to turn the car off.

Test Drive Record

Distance	Time	Velocity

Glossary

Acceleration: The rate of change of velocity; a body can accelerate by changing either its speed or direction.

Action and reaction: Two forces that act whenever an object is moved; the moving force is the *action*, and the object resists or pushes back with a force called *reaction*.

Angle: The shape made when two straight lines meet at a point; the lever of the catapult as it touches the base.

Axle: The shaft that allows wheels to turn; the axle is the wooden dowel in the rubber band-propelled car and the motorcar.

Balance: The act of keeping an object level while suspended in the air by distributing weight equally on each end; equal weights on either side of a fulcrum.

Battery: A device made up of cells that store energy as low-voltage electricity.

Brake: To slow the turning of a wheel by pushing an object against it to cause friction.

Cereal box cardboard: Lightweight, easy-to-cut, stiff, strong cardboard; the same cardboard can also be found in shoeboxes, crayon boxes, and most boxes used to hold food products.

Corrugated cardboard: Rippled paper sandwiched between two sheets of heavy paper. When made into cardboard boxes, it is great for shipping, storing, and packaging. Corrugated cardboard is structurally strong.

Cutting: The act of using a sharp instrument to separate one piece of something into two; takes skill and practice. Take your time and get help when sawing wood, swimming pool noodles, and other materials.

Diameter: The width of a circle.

Dowels: Round or square wooden sticks, usually 36 inches long, found in most hardware and craft stores; most projects work best with 1/4-inch dowels, but if you have an accumulation of chopsticks from Asian restaurants, they work just as well if they are long enough. You can also adjust the project by making it smaller to fit the length of your chopstick.

Drag: The force with which air or water resists the motion of an object such as a car, boat, or aircraft; also called water or air resistance.

Drill: A little hand-crank craft drill works fine for the wood catapult. The car requires a 1/32 bit. But an electric drill operated by an adult is best for projects that may require a lot of drilling. Never use a drill without adult supervision.

Drilling: Boring a hole into an object.

Elasticity: The stretchiness of a rubber band.

Electrical energy: Energy supplied by continuous flow of electrons through a wire or other conductor.

Electrical tape: Protective tape used to tape wires.

Energy: The capacity to do work.

Foam core: Polystyrene sandwiched between two sheets of paper; stiff and strong enough to use for mechanical projects. It is easy to cut with an X-Acto blade or utility knife. Foam core is an excellent, structurally strong material to use as a base for any of the projects. It may curl up slightly after painting.

Force: The pushing and pulling of objects to cause them to move.

Friction: A force that occurs when one thing rubs against another, or when it moves through a liquid or gas.

Fulcrum: The point on which a lever is supported so that it can balance, swing, or tilt, such as the dowel on the catapult.

Glue: An adhesive used to hold two or more objects together. If you have time to let it dry, you can use white glue for everything that the low-temperature hot glue is used for. When decorating projects, you can also add white glue to tempera paint to make the projects stronger. Pour in equal amounts of glue and paint, and then stir with your paintbrush. The multipurpose white glue can be used on paper, wood, cloth, and more.

Engineer This!

Glue gun: An electrical device that heats up sticks of glue. Squeeze the trigger to force glue out of the gun onto the project. The glue cools quickly. A low-temperature mini-glue gun works best on these projects.

Gravity: The force that pulls objects to Earth and causes them to have weight.

Hammer: A hammer is great for pounding nails into objects.

Hole punch: Use a well-made single hole punch to put holes into the projects. Putting holes in plastic containers and cardboard or foam core may take the grip of an adult.

Impellers: Protrusions around an axle used to generate force or receive force.

Inertia: Resistance of a moving object to a change in its speed or direction; the resistance of a stationary object to being moved.

Kinetic energy: Energy created by movement, such as rushing water, wind, or by sound, light, heat, or electromagnetic waves.

Lever: A simple machine with a rigid bar that pivots at the fulcrum to make it easier to lift and move a load.

Masking tape: An easy-to-use tape that is inexpensive and comes in different widths. You can cut it with practically any scissors or tear it with your fingers.

Mass: A measure of an object's inertia, or its heaviness; contrast with weight, which is a measure of gravitational force on an object.

Nail: When putting a nail hole through an object, always put a board or thick cardboard under the object so that the nail does not go into your worktable. We use a nail instead of a drill or when a single hole punch isn't strong enough.

Needle-nose pliers: Pliers used for fine work, such as electrical wiring, jewelry making, and home repairs.

Paint: Acrylic paint is excellent to work with and will stick to all of the surfaces of the projects, but it doesn't wash out of clothes. Tempera paint only sticks to paper products that do not have a gloss coating, and it can stain your clothes. To use tempera, mix glue into it. For structural strength, pour in an equal amount of tempera paint and the white, multi-purpose glue that says it works on paper, wood, cloth, pottery, and more. The glue dries almost clear so it doesn't change the color of the paint much. If I want a nice plastic, glossy look, then I pour in a thick, gooey tacky glue. It is a little harder to paint with, but it gives a nice finish.

Paper tubes: Sometimes you will need a thin paper tube and sometimes you will need a thicker one, but you shouldn't ever need the ones that are so thick that you can't use a hole punch on them. (You should be saving these for your projects as you use them at home.)

Pivot: The turning motion of the lever on the fulcrum.

Pliers: A hand tool used for grasping that operates on a pivot using a lever/fulcrum principal. Needle-nose pliers have a tapered jaw with teeth and a cutting blade at the pivot. Diagonal cutting pliers are no larger than adult scissors, but have a cutting edge that can cut heavy-gauge wire and 1/4-inch dowels.

Polystyrene: A semi-hard, usually white foam used in shipping and packing. It is easy to saw, cut, and poke, depending on its thickness.

Potential energy: Energy that is stored, such as in chemicals, fuels, and food.

Projectile: The object that flies or is thrust through the air.

Pulley: A wheel that holds the drive belt, usually a groove cut into it to hold the belt on.

Range: The distance the projectile flies through the air.

Resistance: A force that slows the movement of an object; see also *drag*.

Rubber bands: The only sizes of rubber bands used in this book are #16 and #18. If you have a box of miscellaneous rubber bands and don't know their sizes, you can measure them: A size #16 is 2 1/2 inches by 1/16 inch, and #18 is 3 inches by 1/16 inch.

Rudder: A movable piece on the back of an airplane or boat.

Safety: Always the most important part of building your project. To avoid mishaps, read the instructions and plan what you are going to do before you get started. Always have an adult present to help you.

Scissors: Adult-size craft scissors are the best to use for the projects. You can also use spring-loaded scissors to cut cardboard. We can't say enough good things about the springy scissors—they save a lot of work for your hands. We have a pair of diagonal-cutting pliers that we use to cut 1/4-inch dowels and craft sticks. We also have a small pair of tin snips, which are perfect for cutting heavy cardboard. The pair we use has sharp, pointy tips and is good for making holes in things that a hole punch will not work on.

Sewing: Inserting string through a hole by means of a stronger, more rigid implement, such as a pipe cleaner or a sewing needle.

Shaft: A wooden stick that allows the wheels to turn.

Speed: The rate at which something moves.

Tension: The degree of tightness of something, usually rubber bands in this book.

Thrust: A sudden forceful push that propels something forward.

Velocity: A speed in a particular direction.

Weight: A measure of gravitational force on an object.

Wheel: A disc that turns on a shaft or axle; may be used as the tires on the motorcar.

Wheel and axle: A class of rotating machines or devices in which effort applied to one part produces a useful movement in another part.

⋀⋀⋀⋀ References

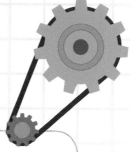

Choi, C. Q. (2015). World's oldest stone tools predate humans. *Live Science*. Retrieved from http://www.livescience.com/50908-oldest-stone-tools-predate-humans.html

Engineering is Elementary. (2017). *The engineering design process*. Retrieved from http://www.eie.org/overview/engineering-design-process

Swenson, P. (2017). History of the jack-in-the-box toy. *How To Adult*. Retrieved from http://howtoadult.com/history-jackinthebox-toy-50 82822.html

Wikipedia. (2017). *Parachute*. Retrieved from https://en.wikipedia.org/wiki/Parachute

About the Authors

In the summer of 1974, and for the first time since World War II, most of the branches of the U.S. military advertised to women. Along with thousands of other women, **Carol J. McBride** signed up. Since then, she has studied engineering and drafting, worked as a traffic engineer, majored in philosophy at the University of Arizona, and learned to draw.

As an arts and crafts instructor, she taught kids how to build mechanical toys out of recyclables and trash, tape, glue, and a little paint, and called the classes "MacGyver" in tribute to the methods used in the television show.

Carol now drives a 200-ton haulage dump truck loaded with 320 tons of copper and dirt—a daily, close-up and personal study of the principles of physics. She wrote and illustrated the earlier iteration of this book, *Making Magnificent Machines: Fun With Math, Science, and Engineering*, and illustrated *It Was a Dark and Stormy Night, It Was a Hot and Steamy Night*, and *It Was a Wild and Crazy Life* by Misa Gonzales.

Engineer This!

Her coauthor and husband, **Francisco Gonzales**, is a clay artist, wood sculptor, and teacher. The only son of a copper miner and folk artist, Pancho spent his life exploring the wilderness and abandoned mines, and the ancient and more modern ruins around his home towns, Morenci, AZ, and Clifton, AZ. After high school, Pancho began working for the Phelps Dodge copper mine. It was at the copper mine that he first encountered high-fire furnaces used in the smelting of metals. He says, "The process is dirty and dangerous, and the scale of the furnace is huge. The furnace was 3,000 degrees and it was my job to maintain the temperature inside—I wore three layers of clothing and a fire suit with a respirator."

Pancho left his hometown and the copper mine and moved to Tucson to major in design at the University of Arizona. He studied clay under Maurice Grossman, and he began to develop his own style. He is also the author and illustrator of the children's books *The Big Stumble* and *When I Say Jump, Jump.*

The engineering projects Carol and Pancho designed together develop problem solving and encourage creativity, sequential thinking, and art and design skills. The projects teach math, science, and engineering through the building of these interesting, hands-on creations.

About the Contributors

Misa Gonzales, editor and literary agent, is an educator, speaker, writer, and author of *It Was a Dark and Stormy Night*, *It Was a Hot and Steamy Night*, and *It Was a Wild and Crazy Life*. She was recognized as a "Champion of Change" at the White House by President Barack Obama in 2013, as one of the top 10 technology-based instructors in the nation. She has two wonderful kids, Zavier and Krysma.

Cassie Gonzales won *Granta*'s one-sentence story competition, *The Kenyon Review*'s Short Fiction Contest, Literary Death Match, and London StorySlam. She was shortlisted for the BBC's International Radio Playwriting Competition and *The Paris Review*'s Flash Fiction Competition, published by *Tin House*, and selected for performance by London's Insignificant Theater and Liars' League: London, Hong Kong, and New York. Her play, *REX*, has been published and produced several times in the U.S. Cassie has also been published by *Sonora Review* and *The McNeese Review*, and is one of the authors in the critically acclaimed *The Letters Page*. Awarded a Fellowship at Emory University, Atlanta, GA, for 2017–2019, she also holds a master's degree in creative writing from the University of Oxford, and lives with her husband, Joe Shea, in Stockholm, Sweden.

Engineer THIS!

Turn trash into invention and sharpen your engineering eye with these 10 hands-on engineering projects. Using recycled and easy-to-find materials, engineer your own motorcar, catapult, glider, and other completely functional machines. Explore amazing scientific concepts, such as potential, kinetic, and electrical energy; principles of flight; weights and balances; pulleys and levers; laws of motion; and more. Each project includes step-by-step instructions, full-color photos, exciting facts, safety tips, and extended engineering and science activities for further discovery.

Please visit our website at
http://www.prufrock.com

Cover design by Raquel Trevino

Printed in the USA

PRUFROCK PRESS INC.™

$14.95 US

-1-61821-629-8
51495

9 781618 216298